The "I" of the Sermon

FORTRESS RESOURCES FOR PREACHING

THE "I" OF THE SERMON
Autobiography in the Pulpit

RICHARD L. THULIN

FORTRESS PRESS   MINNEAPOLIS

Library of Congress Cataloging-in-Publication Data

Thulin, Richard L.
   The "I" of the sermon.

   (Fortress resources for preaching)
   Bibliography: p.
   1. Autobiographical preaching. I. Title. II. Series.
BV4235.A87T48 1989   251   88–45228
ISBN 0–8006–1148–9

3453I88   Printed in the United States of America   1-1148

To
Elizabeth, Geoffrey, Leslie, Kendra,
whose presence has enriched my story beyond measure

Contents

Preface

This book is about the use of personal story in preaching. More specifically, it is about the use of autobiography, of first-person singular narrative as a vehicle for the proclamation of God's Word. The title of the book suggests that the "I" of the sermon is not unlike the "eye" of a storm. Such a suggestion is not an exaggeration—a storm rages around the issue of pulpit autobiography. Many forbid its use altogether. Others warn against its destructive possibilities. Some few support its use, but their voices are almost drowned out by the cries of those who disapprove. Unfortunately, little systematic inquiry has been carried out by either side. Assumptions have gone unquestioned. Claims and counterclaims have gone unchallenged. Personal stories actually told from the pulpit have gone unexamined. This book attempts to provide the kind of inquiry into pulpit autobiography that has been missing. It will certainly not quiet the storm, but it may help lessen the storm's ferocity.

The result of this inquiry is a clear affirmation of personal story as a vehicle for Christian proclamation. It issues in a strong personal conviction that the use of first-person singular narrative can be one of the most effective forms that preaching can assume. I hope that the findings recorded here will provide solid information for preachers who use personal story in their sermons and who want a means of evaluation as well as suggestions for effective use. I also hope that my work will encourage preachers who are intrigued by the use of pulpit autobiography, but who are hesitant to use it for one reason or another. Finally, I hope that my inquiry and conclusions will open possibilities for

9

preachers who have not thought much about personal story in preaching, or who have rejected it outright as a vehicle of proclamation.

Some of the material in this book was first read at meetings of the
Academy of Homiletics. Members of the academy's Section on Narrative Preaching have been particularly helpful in their support and
criticism. I am grateful to them. I am also grateful to the Lutheran
Theological Seminary at Gettysburg, Pennsylvania, for a sabbatical
leave that gave me unhurried time for research and reflection. Schol-
arship assistance from Aid Association for Lutherans and from Lutheran
Brotherhood has greatly eased the financial burden of such an under-
taking.

Lutheran Theological Seminary   RICHARD L. THULIN
Gettysburg, Pennsylvania   Ulrich Professor of the
                                         Art of Preaching

1
The Case for
Personal Story

Reactions to the use of personal stories in the pulpit are easy to come by. Many of these reactions, it must be admitted, are strongly negative. They vary from mild hesitation to outright rejection. Such reactions, informed or otherwise, must be taken seriously. Even those that seem overstated signal a potential danger. Traps await those who choose to share an autobiographical tale from the pulpit.

Many who warn against the use of personal story in the pulpit rightly focus on the purpose of Christian preaching. We are in the pulpit to preach Christ, they insist. If stories are to be a part of Christian proclamation, they assert, such stories must be about Jesus and about what God has revealed and accomplished through him. Such a warning recognizes the inherent power of narrative to engage the listener in a unique way. It also points, however, to a danger inherent in the use of personal story for preaching. Unless it is used appropriately, the personal story can dominate the sermon in such a way that it obstructs Christian proclamation. It is possible for a personal story to call such attention to the preacher that he or she becomes the center of focus. If this happens, the preacher is proclaimed and not Christ. And that would constitute narcissism at its self-aggrandizing worst.

Critics of pulpit autobiography also point to the fact that Christian preaching is always a word to others. It must be a word that places its hearers under the judgment and grace of God. In essence, it is a dialogic word and not a monologic one. It is clearly possible for the personal story to fall into the trap of privatism. The tale shared may be so idiosyncratic that the listener finds it impossible to make connections

11

between the preacher's story and his or her own. If this occurs, the preacher is no longer preaching. The sermon has become nothing more than a public form of self-expression. The listeners are placed as eavesdroppers to secrets they did not want to hear and about which they do not know what to do.

The isolation of the preacher's story from the stories of the congregation is a very real danger. So is the isolation of the preacher's story from the rest of the sermon and from the biblical text that provides the basis for the sermon. Complaints against pulpit autobiography often focus on this isolation: "What in the world did that tale have to do with the rest of the sermon?" "Where in the world did that story connect with the biblical story?" What really bothers those who level such complaints is that the rest of the sermon and the biblical story usually suffer from such isolation. Listeners remember the isolated tale and forget what was to have been the main point.

The dangers of narcissism, privatism, and isolation are real. To fall prey to any or all of them is not a matter of indifference. Each militates against the nature and purpose of Christian preaching. Some preachers may be unaware of these dangers, but others are so aware of them that they refuse to even consider personal story as a sermonic option. Still other preachers are aware of the dangers to the extent that they are inhibited from acting on the attraction they feel for autobiographical narrative. As real as the dangers are, however, they should not keep preachers from exploring the possibilities of personal story. Nor should such dangers be allowed to ban personal story from the pulpit. The traps are not inevitable—they can be avoided. It is possible for personal story to proclaim Christ, to place its hearers under the judgment and grace of God, to be an integral part of the sermon, and to accurately express the biblical text. The traps are not inevitable. They can be avoided through awareness, skill, and practice.

Gaining even partial mastery over the use of personal story for preaching is well worth the effort. Some of us have learned that pulpit autobiography offers dividends far beyond what we ever imagined. A personal tale can do far more than add a note of human interest to the sermon or arrest the straying attention of an audience. The use of pulpit autobiography can help bolster the sagging authority of the pulpit. It does so, in part, by placing the preacher where she or he needs to stand in relation to the tradition and community of the church.

PERSONAL STORY AND AUTHORITY

I learned something crucial about a preacher's authority as far back as my intern year as a seminary student. For twelve months I served as an assistant in a five-church parish and as an associate chaplain in a small church-sponsored hospital. My first visit to a patient was to an elderly woman confined to the bed of a private room. I had not had formal training in pastoral care and felt somewhat uneasy, yet I was sure that my youthful exuberance would carry the day. Enthusiastically I entered the room, introduced myself, and asked the woman how she was feeling. Her answer came in two words: "I'm dying." I was not at all certain how to respond and I did the only thing that came to mind. I asked her how she knew that she was dying. Again, her answer was brief. "My doctor told me," she said. I think I mumbled, "I'm sorry," because I could manage nothing else. Suddenly, the woman asked me a question. "Son," she said, "do you believe that there is life after death?" My mind raced and my tongue did its best to keep up. I quoted the Bible, bits and pieces from what I could recall from a course in dogmatics, and just about anything else that popped into my head. In the middle of my rambling, the woman took my hand. She said, "Son, that's all very nice—but that isn't what I asked you. What I need to know is whether or not *you* believe that there is life after death." That woman contributed to my understanding of ministry and its authority more than she could ever imagine. She gave me one of the greatest gifts I have ever received. She forced me to speak out of my own Christian experience, out of my own tumultuous life of faith and doubt.

In that hospital room I discovered what I have repeatedly discovered in the pulpit. In preaching, as in other forms of pastoral ministry, the preacher cannot hide. People demand a clear and honest word from the one who speaks. That demand will not be met by a barrage of Bible verses or by a host of brilliant quotations from recognized theologians. That demand will be met only when the preacher speaks the truth out of his or her own life.

I do not remember exactly what I said to the hospitalized woman who asked me to speak out of my own belief. I am sure that I did not share a well-crafted story from my life experience. No doubt I spoke in bits and pieces. I am almost certain, however, that I was working toward an autobiographical narrative. I remember, for example, telling her about the death of my grandmother—the telephone call in the middle of the night, the hushed voices of my mother and father, my child's reaction to the simple words, "Grandma is dead." I know that I told her of my prayers thanking God that "Grandma is with you forever," and of my lively expectation that Grandma and I will be together again beyond all separation. And I remember that when I left her room the dying woman said, "Thank you. You told me what I needed to hear."

From that woman I learned the crucial fact that a preacher's authority is a personal authority. This may not always have been as obvious as it is in the contemporary world. People will not listen seriously to what a minister says simply because he or she is ordained and speaks with the authority of the church. Nor will people be receptive to what a minister says simply because she or he quotes from the Bible or from the writings of some significant theologian. What catches the ear and urges response is the voice of a living witness. What is needed is the voice of one who can testify to the accuracy of what he or she speaks. Not because it has been read somewhere or because it has been over-heard, but because it speaks the truth about one's own life, and because it speaks the truth from the details of one's own life. It is a voice of conviction supported by a life story.

Authority is more readily granted to preachers who attempt to honestly connect personal life with the biblical and theological tradition. Authority is less readily granted to preachers who simply talk about their lives per se. It is granted to preachers who can talk from their own lives in terms of the presence and activity of God attested to by Scripture and theology alike. Such a granting of authority is not strange. Preaching is the self-expression of the church. In its preachers the church becomes conscious of itself as the inheritor of a tradition and as the living witness to that tradition. The preacher represents both the tradition and a present community of the faithful. On behalf of the tradition, the preacher introduces, clarifies, amplifies, and asserts what it is that the church believes. On behalf of the congregation, the preacher examines the tradition and questions the experiential grounds for continuing to believe the church's faith. When this happens, the church is most clearly part of a living tradition. When this happens, the church is at its self-conscious best.

By using personal story, a preacher can effectively fulfill his or her task as representative of both tradition and congregation. Personal story enables one to show what is believed and to demonstrate why this is the case. To be sure, this means sharing a personal opinion about the inherited tradition. Personal opinion, however, does not necessitate privatism. Indeed, if the preacher serves as representative of the congregation as well as of the tradition, her or his voice will not be idiosyncratic.

Part of the preacher's responsibility to speak as a representative of the congregation is met by examining the tradition and providing clues for the experiential basis for its claims. Another part of that same task is to speak from the common life to the common life. Many preachers have discovered that personal story is a fit vehicle for such speech. Personal story can effectively demonstrate that the preacher knows what it is like to be human in that time and place. Personal story can assure a congregation that they have been listened to and heard, that their hopes and their fears, their successes and their failures, their faithfulness and their neglect are placed firmly within the church's tradition. Personal story can lend a unique credibility and thus establish a preacher's authority as one "who knows what it's like."

PERSONAL STORY AND THE PREACHER

Personal story can constitute an authoritative word and thus assist effective pulpit proclamation. In addition, the process by which personal stories are selected and crafted can offer substantial benefits to the individual preacher. For example, the process connecting life story with church tradition is a theological activity. The preacher who struggles to establish such a relationship is functioning as a theologian. She or he is working to make sense of inherited truth, to find reciprocal access between the faith and experienced human life. Theological thinking involves more than repeating crystallized statements of doctrine. It involves sensing the human experience out of which doctrine arises and for which doctrine should serve as a catalyst. An attempt to interweave personal story and church tradition enables preachers to actively engage their theological task.

Some years ago a student in one of my classes preached a sermon on justification by grace through faith. He repeated all the right concepts in a nicely structured presentation. Both he and the class felt that he had fulfilled his theological task with distinction. During class discussion of the sermon, I asked the student preacher if he could tell us what it felt like to be justified. "I don't understand what you mean," he said. "Well," I responded, "you have just spent twenty minutes telling us about God's justifying act. We assume that you have experienced that act. Simply tell us about it. What difference, for example, has it made in your life?"

Only after considerable reflection was the student able to give an answer. He did so by telling us of a violent breakfast argument between himself and his wife. He left his home so angry that he did not care if he ever saw his wife again. During the day he came to realize that he had provoked the argument. His mood changed from anger to fear. He grew fearful of going home, certain that his wife would not be there or that she would be withdrawn and beyond reach. It was after dark when he nervously opened the front door. His wife heard him and came running. She threw her arms around his neck, kissed him, and said, "Welcome home!"

"Is that," the student asked, "what you had in mind?" I did not have to say a word. The class was overwhelmed. "Why didn't you say that in the sermon?" someone asked. "That's what I call bringing the theological truth to life," said another. Both were right. The student had talked theology in the sermon. He did not do theology, however, until he began to connect God's gift of undeserved grace with that gift of grace offered him by his wife.

When preachers do theology by connecting life story and church tradition they receive a benefit beyond the satisfaction of performing an essential task. Week by week, for an entire lifetime, they can work at retrieving their own stories and seeing them in the light of God's work. For many, this has been the major spiritual discipline and the center of their growth in faith. They understand that the very nature of the preaching task calls them to notice their own lives, to evaluate them in light of the judgment and grace of God, and to reshape them in line with what God has revealed.

For several years, I have required students in my preaching classes to focus on their personal response to biblical texts. I ask them to share with the rest of us their emotional, intellectual, and behavioral responses. I invite them to share recollections, incidents recalled by association with what the biblical text says and does. I am always surprised by the variety and range of the recall. I am more surprised, though, by the blessing that such a simple exercise seems to be. Some students claim that they rarely receive such an invitation. Few people seem interested in what sense, if any, the students are making out of their lives in terms of God. Thus they are delighted by the chance to remember and share. Most of all, though, the students are amazed by what the texts release to their consciousness. Events long forgotten are remembered. People and places long out of sight appear. Words long muffled are heard once again. Such anamnesis is a blessing in itself. But the texts that serve as catalyst for the memory also interpret and contextualize what is remembered. The texts provide eyes and ears by which the recalled can be seen and heard in a new way. The texts invite rememberers to comprehend their daily lives as places where God actively works. And the students find themselves blessed again.

There are preachers who carry out this kind of dialogue between text and personal life week after week. They do it in preparation for preaching. They also do it as a way of centering themselves, of keeping themselves alive to the presence and work of God in their own lives and beyond. Attentive to their own stories, they become more attentive to the stories of others. Aware of the presence of God in their own lives, they become more aware of God's presence in the lives of others. Many preachers have told me that this kind of dialogue is so important to them that they would continue it even if they were to stop preaching. It gives them back their own lives and connects them to others. It reveals God as the center of every life.

2
Types of
Personal Story

The preacher who uses personal story in preaching has more than one option from which to choose. Several types of first-person singular narrative have been used by preachers past and present. My study of sermonic material, for example, reveals four such types—illustration, reminiscence, confession, and self-portrayal—which can be clearly distinguished from one another in terms of content, function, and degree of self-disclosure. Understanding them can help a preacher decide the way in which a personal story is to be told from the pulpit and can also aid a preacher in analyzing the sermonic stories of others.

PERSONAL STORY AS ILLUSTRATION

I describe illustration as a brief first-person singular narrative used to clarify or confirm a general statement. Such illustrations are usually based on memories of childhood and family, or on events recalled from one's ministry or travel. They are used because a statement already made needs explanation or experiential support. Most often, they reveal little of the person whose story it is and lack those details that invite the listener to participate in the shared incident. Illustrations exist to serve the general statement; self-revelation and detail only get in the way. While illustrations of this sort utilize the first-person singular and personal experience, they are minimally autobiographical. No more is known about the preacher, where he stands or how she knows what she knows, after the illustration than before.

Karl Barth's sermons do not contain many personal stories. There are some, however. In his sermon "You Shall Be My People," there appears a good example of what I have described.[1] Barth asserts that God's yes to us is a holy and wholesome yes, comprising always a no. Then he attempts to clarify that general statement by an analogy: "He treats us like a doctor who prescribes pills and medication we utterly dislike."[2] Barth then briefly recalls that, as a boy, he had to drink a glass of cod-liver oil every morning. "It tasted terrible, but it obviously did me some good," he writes. Barth's personal reference is made in the service of the assertion that God's yes comprises a no. If the illustration has explained the assertion, then we can forget it. The personal story has no life of its own and no tale to tell on its own; without the assertion that precedes it, it has little significance. And it must be said that the personal story is not very personal. Barth tells us what he thinks we need to know in order to make his point, but certainly the details could have been extended considerably. Did he need cod-liver oil because he was sickly, or because it was a custom? Did his parents have to force him to drink it? If so, which parent? Did he ever flush it down the toilet when no one was looking, as I remember doing when I was a boy? How bad did it taste? When did he come to realize that it was a beneficial tonic? How did he feel about the no of cod-liver oil encompassed by the yes of parental care? Barth does not come close to answering these questions and others. If he had answered them, we would learn more about Barth than we already know, but we might also forget the point about God's yes and no. The story, then, would have failed its function. Personal story as illustration attends the general assertion.

PERSONAL STORY AS REMINISCENCE

I describe the reminiscence as a rather detailed first-person singular narrative which tells its own story and is clearly significant to the teller. I have worded the description in this way in order to distinguish reminiscence from illustration. In several ways, of course, they are quite similar. Both are narratives of things remembered, persons or incidents, and are usually concerned with private relationships rather than with public events. Both recount "things of memory," even though on occasion illustration may tell of a current incident. In other ways, however, illustration and reminiscence are markedly different. The reminiscence, for example, includes more detail in the telling than does the illustration. Normally this detail conveys emotional content and the reminiscence then has a tonal quality that the illustration does not. The reader/listener gets the feeling that the incident has more significance to the teller than being one example, among many, of a general assertion: Whatever message the reminiscence conveys, the message is more inherent in the story told than it is laid alongside of that story. If the listener forgets the story, the listener will forget the message; the message is in the story.

It has often been pointed out that the only unusual feature of the typically medieval sermons of Hugh Latimer was the "strain of autobiographical allusion and reminiscence."[3] In Latimer's "First Sermon preached before King Edward the Sixth" (1549) appears the famous paragraph that begins, "My father was a yeoman, and has no lands of his own."[4] The personal reference that follows is instructive as a narrative reminiscence as well as a reflection of conditions in sixteenth-century England. The reminiscence is part of an appeal for redress of "all such proceedings which . . . do intend plainly to make the yeomanry slavery, and the clergy slavery." It illustrates the need for reform by asserting the fact that yeoman have become slaves. It does more, however, than provide an informative instance. Latimer does not say that he is angry or distressed by the change in circumstances, but the listener knows how he feels all the same. The details of the account convey a poignancy that may be far more persuasive than anger. There is both gratitude and satisfaction in the memory of what his father had been able to do for the king, for himself, for his children, and for the poor, as one who "had no lands of his own," only "a farm of three. or four pound by year at the uttermost." And there is sadness that the same possibilities no longer exist, where he that now has the farm "payeth sixteen pound by year, or more, and is not able to do anything for his prince, for himself, nor for his children, or give a cup of drink to the poor." The significance of the recollection for Latimer is suggested by the fact that his memory is not of a single incident but of a condition or state in which many incidents coalesce. Latimer has gained a perspective on that condition or state, a perspective provided in part by the length of the intervening years. Any general statement served by the reminiscence seems to be inherent in the account itself. That is, the listener would probably "get the point" even if Latimer did not state it in other terms.

PERSONAL STORY AS CONFESSION

Before defining what I mean by confession, I want to indicate what is not included in my use of the term. It does not include statements of personal conviction, however moving and convincing those statements may be. James S. Stewart's thunderous claim, "I know whom I have believed—I know His promise stands fast forever," does not qualify.[5] It does not include confessions of guilt or complicity in sin, regardless of how honest or confessional those concessions are. Karl Barth's admission, "I include myself—I stand ready to confess being the greatest sinner among you all," does not qualify.[6] The focus here must be on narrative. No matter how personal statements of conviction or admissions of guilt may be, they are not narrative in form.

I choose to define confession as a personal recounting of a spiritual experience. In terms of the history of religious autobiography, a confession will probably tell of the frightful struggles of the soul, the "final convincement of salvation," or the workings of God's providence in vocation or personal life.[7] Like the illustration, the confession usually offers few details and recounts an experience that is highly significant for the narrator.

There are also dissimilarities between the confession and both the illustration and the reminiscence. While the illustration tends to focus on the truth of a general statement, and while the reminiscence tends to focus on the memory of the one who remembers, the confession focuses on the self. As Georges Gusdorf has indicated, the "confession takes on the character of . . . a recognition of the self by the self."[8] Its concern is to announce one's place before God.[9] It seeks "to communicate or express the essential nature, the truth, of the self" in its relation to God.[10] The portrayal of the self in its relationship to God further sets the confession apart from the reminiscence. While the reminiscence usually reveals the narrator in private relationship with family or friends, the confession reveals the narrator in an often intense engagement with God. As a result of this focus, the narrator in the confession is often drained of individuality and history. Usually there is no reference to either the workings of the narrator's mind or the cultural context in which the engagement with God occurred.

The confession can be further distinguished from the illustration and the reminiscence by its intention. The function of the illustration is to clarify or explain. The purpose of the reminiscence is most frequently to make an appeal. The confession intends as much as anything the setting forth of an example; the narrator becomes an exemplar. The narrator hopes that his or her own "soul history" will provide incentive or pattern for Christian belief, action, and attitude for others.[11]

In his sermon "Why People Don't Go to Church," Leslie Weatherhead relates a remembered moment of spiritual intensity.[12] In the sermon, Weatherhead claims that people go to church to find forgiveness. He asserts that only those for whom sin is real ("some burdened spirit, some depressed heart, some crushed soul") are "caught up joyously, gladly, volitionally, into the perfect harmony with God" which is forgiveness.[13] He draws a distinction between knowing the fact that God forgives sins and knowing forgiveness experientially. Then he tells of his own experience of forgiveness one Easter Sunday night in a crowded YMCA tent during World War II.

The narration includes few details. There is no indication of the year except that it was during the war. There is no indication of the place except that Weatherhead was a "staff officer riding from one Arab sheik to another on government business." It is perhaps more significant that there is no disclosure of Weatherhead's state of mind or spirit. He does say that he had not been able to attend a service for weeks. But we do not know whether he was burdened in spirit, depressed in heart, or crushed in soul. The general context suggests that such may have been the case but we do not know.

It was during the singing of the hymn "Christ the Lord Is Risen Today" that Weatherhead says God's presence became a fact. While he refers to the moment as "rapture" and suggests that it offered an incomparable sense of unity with God, he finds the moment difficult to describe in ordinary language. What he experienced, he says, is "something of what John Wesley felt . . . in Aldersgate Street," and it is what Masefield writes about in his poem "The Everlasting Mercy." Both references are charged emotionally and suggest the significance of the moment for Weatherhead. There remains, however, a certain ineffability and inaccessibility about the occurrence as well as about the event or state leading into it. In neither case do we know from the inside, as it were, exactly what happened. The focus is clearly on the person of Weatherhead, but the identity of that person stays clouded. Nor do we see the outcome of the experience. Weatherhead suggests that it made a difference to him, and the excerpt from Masefield's poem suggests that the felt unity with God extended itself to a sense of unity with "all earthly creatures" and creations. But we do not really know. Weatherhead centers on his relationship with God. What was different for him in terms of human relationships or relationships with the world of nature and culture is left to conjecture.

The purpose of Weatherhead's personal confession seems to extend beyond that of an illustration or appeal. This is the case even though it serves as an example of the "endless offer" of God's forgiveness and as an encouragement to faith by one who is "offering in the Name of Christ that miracle." It appears to be offered also as a pattern for belief, action, and attitude. Weatherhead provides incentive toward a duplication of his own experience. He encourages the listener not by some conclusion he has drawn from a remembered event, but by the remembered event itself.

PERSONAL STORY AS SELF-PORTRAYAL

I describe self-portrayal as first-person singular narrative which focuses on the self as thinking, feeling, and willing, and on the self in the totality of its relationships. It is the most comprehensive form of first-person narrative. It includes key aspects of both the reminiscence and the confession and unites their varying emphases while often moving beyond them. Such a description of self-portrayal is dependent upon studies on the nature of autobiography. Ray Pascal, for example, speaks for many when he identifies as the distinction of great autobiography the "truth of being, an integration and reunion of different aspects of the person, a coherence of acting and the spiritual personality in the particularity of circumstances."[14] I have translated this as a focus on the self as thinking, feeling, and willing. Marcus Billson and Sidonie Smith speak for others also when they indicate that autobiography is the story of a person's unfolding sense of identity, the tale of becoming in the world.[15] I have translated this as a focus on the self in the totality of its relationships. Self-portrayal seeks precise observation of both the inner and outer world and it attempts to relate them meaningfully.

The focus of the narrative of self-portrayal is similar to that of the reminiscence inasmuch as it exhibits the self as thinking. It is similar to the confession inasmuch as it reveals the self as feeling. It moves beyond both, however, in showing the self as willing. Whatever story is told, it includes some idea of what difference the related events have made to the narrator. Life is not the same for the narrator as it was before. A different, or altered, determination and set of actions flow from what has happened and been told.

The narrative of self-portrayal in preaching includes the emphasis of the reminiscence on the self in its relationship with other selves and culture, and it includes the confession's emphasis on the self in its relationship with God. It also combines the reminiscence's function as appeal and the confession's purpose of example or pattern. It moves beyond both, however, in envisioning friendship or companionship as one of its goals. Lawrence Sterne may speak for many portrayers of the self: "As you proceed further with me, the slight acquaintance which is now beginning betwixt us, will grow into familiarity; and that, unless one of us is at fault, will terminate in friendship."[16]

With companionship as its goal, the narrative of self-portrayal best fulfills the preacher's need as a confessor. While preachers represent their communities in their preaching, they also need to confirm their identity narrative. Self-portrayal invites and evokes the understanding, confirmation, and prayers of the community to a greater degree than the other narrative forms.

Like the reminiscence, and unlike the confession and the illustration, the narrative of self-portrayal usually offers a substantial number of details. In part, this increased detailing makes the portrayal more story-like and enables it to participate in what I call the story's "uncanny ability to engage and move those who hear it." The details help create a world, and it is a world that listeners can enter safely because it is both like and unlike that of their daily routine. The personal story enables the inner counterpart of the listener to be externalized. Parishioners have responded to my own use of personal story with the admission, "I can't help listening when you put it that way." The story they heard was not their own, yet they participated in it, made connections with it, and drew some conclusions for their own lives. A personal story, Elizabeth Bowen suggests, "provides the visionary element, in whose light all things told appear momentous and fresh— though they may not be new, though they may have happened before."[17]

It should be clear also that the narrative of self-portrayal can best demonstrate that the preacher knows what he or she is talking about.

I have claimed that the preacher's personal story lies at the heart of the pulpit presence of the "I." Whether that presence appears in the form of declaration, or in the assumption of responsibility, or in the surrender of oneself to the content and dynamics of the sermon, it must locate its identity in personal story. Preachers, I have suggested, will not even know what they are talking about unless what they say is consciously anchored in their own stories. Because the narrative of self-portrayal is the form most storylike, the form with the most detail, it is the form by which preachers can most fully bear witness; by which they can tell as honestly and completely as possible their own experience of a given event.

Personal story as self-portrayal need not be an extended tale. (See appendix 1, pages 77–78 for the text on which the following discussion is based.) In his sermon "The Stranger," for example, Edmund Steimle recalls an incident that had taken place some thirty years earlier.[18] The incident centers on an exchange between Steimle and Mr. Birnbaum, a Jewish tailor married to a Christian woman. The tailor asks Steimle whether or not he should send food to his wife's brother, a "violent Nazi when we were in Germany" who "hated me and did nothing to help us," but who is now in a prison camp. The tailor informs Steimle that while his wife, the Christian, insists that no food should be sent, he, the Jewish tailor, feels that it should be.

While the incident is told with great economy, certain items are nicely detailed. We are told, for example, the tailor's name, that he spoke in a thick accent, and that the setting was the "shop of a friendly neighborhood tailor." The question to Steimle is posed in dialogue form and the problem is presented deftly and forcefully; it remains a personal question and in no way becomes a hypothetical case for passive reflection. Steimle doesn't tell us what response he gave to the tailor, or whether he gave one at all. Rather, he focuses our attention on his internal reaction, not so much to the tailor's question as to the situation out of which the question came. He tells us that he felt ashamed, "ashamed of his Christian wife possibly, but even more ashamed of myself for being unprepared to find the stranger God recognizable on the lips of a pleasant Jewish neighborhood tailor."

In this paragraph-long narrative, Steimle portrays himself as both feeling and thinking. In a later paragraph he reveals a self that wills when he suggests that we can come to bless God because God does come as the stranger into our lives. Steimle makes connections for us between his inner and outer worlds; he shows himself in relationship to both other people and God. Even though he does not tell us the nature of God's presence, we can assume that it is one of judgment and grace.

It is probably dangerous to guess at Steimle's motivation in narrating this incident beyond the fact that it strongly reinforces his claim about the unrecognizable presence of God. But certainly an incident remembered for thirty years must have been memorable and it must have been the point of some enlarging of vision, or the moment of a *metanoia*. Indeed, Steimle indicates that he discovered as though for the first time something he already knew. It may well be that the inclusion of this narrative is a way for Steimle to put the incident finally to rest by putting it in a definitive framework. Perhaps only now is the event somehow concluded, its meanings crystallized and reconciliation effected by admission and disclosure. Even though few listeners are probably able to identify with the remembered incident itself, many readers should be able to identify with Steimle's perplexity, shame, and surprise. And if any counterparts in the experiences of readers are caused to vibrate, then Steimle's discovery can be both education and catharsis.

A somewhat longer and more famous personal story was shared by Martin Luther King, Jr., in his sermon "Our God Is Able."[19] (See appendix 2, pages 79–81, for the text on which the following discussion is based.) After suggesting that we should not wish to surrender the conviction that God is able in spite of the presence of evil and doubts, King points to three areas where God is noticeably able. God can sustain the physical universe; God can subdue all the powers of evil; and God can give individual people inner resources to confront life's trials. In support of this last claim, King appropriately shares a personal story.

Dr. King begins his story by admitting that the first twenty-four years of his life were "packed with fulfillment." Not until he became a part of the Montgomery bus protest was he confronted with the trials of life. Bit by bit, King came to realize that the threatening phone calls and letters which he received in increasing numbers were "in earnest." He became apprehensive and began to waver. One night, he said, all of his fears came down on him at once. At the end of a demanding day he was startled, awakened by a phone call: "Listen, nigger, we've taken all we want from you. Before next week you'll be sorry you ever came to Montgomery."[20] King could not sleep. He got up from bed, paced about the house, heated coffee. Finally, exhausted and with his courage almost gone, he bowed in prayer: "I am at the end of my powers. I have nothing left. . . . I can't face it alone." At that moment, King said, he experienced the presence of the Divine as never before. He heard the quiet assurance of an inner voice. His fears began to leave and his uncertainty disappeared. Three nights later his home was bombed. "Strangely enough," he said, "I accepted the word of the bombing calmly." God had given him the inner resources to face the storm.

In this brief episode of self-portrayal we encounter Martin Luther King, Jr., as a thinking, feeling, and willing person. We see him struggling mentally with the dissonance between twenty-four years of fulfillment and serious threats against his life. We see him exhausted, afraid, helpless, renewed. His emotional reaction to what was happening is both stated and made visual. We know how afraid and apprehensive he was because we can see him sleepless, moving through the kitchen without purpose, bowing in surrender. We also see what difference the assurance he felt made. It was put to the test when his home was bombed.

While King is the only "character" in the story, he connects his inner and outer worlds dramatically. The "trials" he confronted are not abstract. At first occasional telephone calls and letters, they culminate in a human voice breaking the night's silence with, "Listen nigger . . . ." At each point he shows us a picture of what is happening to him inside and out. The story also shows us King in his relationship with God. One who never had to question God's ability to provide inner resources finds himself bowed in prayer over a kitchen table, his own body forming a kind of question mark. We sense the presence of God in the disappearance of King's uncertainty and in the words of an "inner voice." The one led to question ends with confident knowledge that God is more able than he ever imagined or needed to imagine.

It seems clear that Dr. King intends to make an appeal to his audience by means of this story. The introduction to the sermon places that audience in a place different from where he had been for the first twenty-four years of his life. That is, they are people who confront trials and tribulations and who may be either immobilized by fear or helplessly pacing in the dark. He also speaks to them as those whose future may well include nights "darker than a thousand midnights." To such an audience he offers his own story and its concluding affirmation. He knows whereof he speaks. "Let this affirmation," he cries, "be our ringing cry." And he offers them his example. Between the tormenting question of God's ability and the new assurance, there is the image of a man bowed in prayer. There is the key—"I've come to the point where I can't face it alone."

Not as clear, perhaps, is what may be guessed as Dr. King's intention of companionship, his need to be recognized and confirmed by his own community. I am reminded of the personal story shared by South African Allan Boesak following the discovery of a plan to assassinate him.[21] He felt that he needed to explain why he could not stop his activities even though many asked and begged him to. "Many of you were disturbed," he writes, "so disturbed that my wife and I decided that I should speak about it. Hence this sermon."[22] It seems quite possible that this same concern motivated Dr. King to share his story. It is the need to explain to those with whom he identifies why it is that he continues on what seems a life-threatening path. It is important that they understand and accept both him and his ministry.

It is helpful at this point to compare and contrast the four types of personal story just described. At the risk of some oversimplification, I have done this in chart form in chapter 7 (see the table on p. 76). Personal story as self-portrayal is the most comprehensive form of first-person narrative. The rest of this book will deal with the possibilities and problems of this form.

3
Essential Guidelines for Self-Portrayal

In the previous chapter I contrasted self-portrayal with three other prominent forms of first-person singular narrative. Certain features of this description now need to be highlighted. They serve as essential guidelines. When they are present in the personal story, we can feel secure that the story is one of self-portrayal rather than one of illustration, reminiscence, or confession. They also function as safeguards against certain dangers inherent in any tale of self-disclosure.

DISCOVERY

One essential component of story as self-portrayal is the narrator's sense of discovery. The event told needs to have been the instrument of some change of direction or vision for the narrator, who then makes clear both the substance and significance of the change. Without such an acknowledged discovery, the form of the narrative will be something other than self-portrayal. If Edmund Steimle's story of his encounter with Mr. Birnbaum, for example, had ended with the tailor's question, the narrative could not be called one of self-portrayal. It might have served as an effective reminiscence, leading perhaps to a consideration of Christian ethics. But without Steimle's stated discovery of the "unrecognizable presence of God," there would have been insufficient self-disclosure and self-reflection on his part. Failing to state his discovery, Steimle might also have fallen prey to the charge of self-aggrandizement. Without the acknowledgment of God's unrecognizable presence on Steimle's part, we would be left with an image of him as confidant of tailors, friendly professor accessible to problem-ridden people. The acknowledgment, however, connects the personal incident with a more profound reality. Steimle learned something in the encounter, something about the tailor, about himself, and about God. The final focus of the story is not on Steimle as a personality, but on his discovery. Indeed, the story ends by pointing away from Steimle to God.

In a rare moment of sermonic self-portrayal, Theodore Ferris tells how he moved from preaching without manuscript and notes to writing his "notes, the outline, on a little card."[1] Ferris's introduction to the narrative suggests that an illustration will follow; indeed, he says, "To illustrate I am going to . . . ." But what follows is clearly more in the nature of self-portrayal. Ferris writes that for twelve years his preaching without manuscript and notes was coupled with "natural nervousness," "anxiety," and "fear"—the "anxiety of fearing that I might forget the outline." He began, he says, to question why he was doing this to himself. After some reflection he discovered that his reason had little to do with a more adequate proclamation of the gospel. What he came to see was that he kept up the anxiety-producing routine for his own satisfaction—"it was the kind of feat that I was proud of." The recognition and admission of that fact became for Ferris the source of change: "From that time on I wrote my notes . . . and relieved that much of the unnecessary anxiety of preaching." Clearly the key to Ferris's story is not to be found in the apparently simple fact that he changed his manner of sermon delivery, whether or not that change relieved him of an increasing fear. The key is located rather in the self-discovery that gave birth to the change. Without that key the story may have been good material for a preacher's conference on preaching, but it would not have been a narrative of self-portrayal. Ferris does not end his tale by leaving us to feel glad for him but wondering what the story has to do with us. He extends his discovery to the responsibility-burdened members of his audience. It is possible, he asserts, to let go by letting God care for the things God cares about.

The element of discovery is absolutely essential if the personal story is to point beyond the teller and thus offer a word to others. I have come to use personal story more and more in my own preaching. But I remind myself constantly that none of my stories has a place in the pulpit if it has not been of an event through which I have discovered something about myself, others, and God. A couple of years ago, I was asked to preach at the eucharistic service held on graduation day at the seminary where I teach. The assigned text was Isa. 42:1–9. In my preparation I found I could not move past v. 3: "A bruised reed he will not break, and a dimly burning wick he will not quench." Each time I read those words I was transported back almost twenty years to the final weeks of ministry in my first parish. During those weeks three young people died, one of Hodgkins disease, one of pneumonia, and one of meningitis. I thought of their families and of myself, all bruised reeds and dimly burning wicks. I desperately wanted to share the story of those days with the graduating class, almost all of whom would soon be serving parishes as ordained pastors. In true graduation style, I think my initial reason for wanting to tell the story was to let the class know that "things can get rough out there"—just in case they had missed learning that during internship and in their studies! To be honest, I think I also wanted to let the families of the graduates know that the academician before them knew firsthand about pastoring. Neither of these reasons seemed good enough. The first did not seem important enough to bother with and the second was too close to being the ticket for an ego trip. I kept asking myself, But what did you *learn* during those weeks? Did you *learn* anything? In order to answer myself I had to relive the visits of those days: to houses, hospitals, funeral homes, and cemeteries. I had to recall my own tears, tears of anger and sorrow and frustration over my incapacity to say, or do, or be what was needed to make whole. Gradually, I began to refocus on what I had learned. I learned that God keeps the promise spoken through Isaiah: "He [the servant] will not fail or be discouraged" (v. 4). If in any way I fulfilled the task of those weeks, it was only because "God took me by the hand and kept me" (v. 6). I also learned that it is God, not I, who keeps the bruised reed from breaking and the dimly burning wick from being quenched. God keeps the promise made, in spite of our incapacities and "uselessness." I wanted the graduates to participate in these lessons and insights. I wanted them, along with me, to "sing to the Lord a new song" (v. 10). And so I told the story and shared what I had learned and how.

John Killinger speaks for many who write about personal story and preaching. Killinger warns against stories that place the preacher in a favorable light. "Any story," he claims, "that represents the preacher in an awkward or failing or fully human light is potentially helpful to the cause of the sermon."[2] It is difficult to argue with this claim on the

basis of examples offered here. All three preachers show themselves
in a moment of weakness. We see Steimle as ashamed because of an
unforgiving Christian, but even more so because of his own unpre-
paredness to find the stranger God. We see Ferris anxiety-ridden and
proud. We see Thulin angry and impotent. No halo hovers above the
heads of these three preachers. And that is exactly the way that it
should be. As Walter Wangerin, Jr., insists, "the complete drama of
God begins with my rebellion."[3]

Reflection on these sermonic examples, however, suggests that Killinger (still speaking for many others) has not said enough. Steimle
may be ashamed, but he nonetheless encounters God. Ferris remains
neither anxiety-ridden nor proud. I am able to announce God's strength
at work in my weakness. None of us ends his story as one left in failure.
We have been lifted out. That too is part of the story that needs to be
told. The complete drama of God may begin with our rebellion, but
it ends with God's forgiveness. The stories are not simply stories of sin
confessed. They are also stories of faith confessed. And, as Wangerin
insists, "There is no pride in such personal revelation"; "How could
. . . I find personal glory in what amounts to confession."[4] Such stories,
of course, still do not place the preacher in a favorable light. But they
do allow God to appear in a favorable light, as the One who keeps
promises and lifts people out of shame and anxiety and impotence. To
limit the personal story to the negative is finally to fail in honoring
God.

THE WHOLE PERSON

A second essential component of the narrative of self-portrayal is a
focus on the self as thinking, feeling, and willing. Self-portrayal is the
arena of internal history, and, as H. Richard Niebuhr has insisted, "In
internal history our concern is with subject."[5] Here "what is given is
always an '-ing,' a know*ing*, a will*ing*, a believ*ing*, a feel*ing*"; it will tell
"what happened to a self that had lived in darkness and now saw again
trees and the sunrise, children's faces and the eyes of a friend."[6]

It is obvious that any preacher is present to his or her audience as
a full person, and that the different aspects of his or her person are
available to observation. "Personal hints have been left bare," as D.
W. Cleverley Ford puts it, whether or not the preacher intends such
nudity.[7] Attention here, however, is on intentional self-disclosure and

the presentation of the self in first-person narrative form. Both of these are necessary. Certainly there can be intentional disclosures of the self apart from narrative and there can be narratives without intentional personal disclosure. But to have only one of the two present is to have a form other than narrative self-portrayal.

It is far more difficult to find narratives in published sermons disclosing an integration of different aspects of the self than it is to find narratives disclosing only one or two. Examples of the latter are relatively plentiful. One instance is in a sermon by Leslie Weatherhead. The sermon is entitled "The Significance of Silence," and in it Weatherhead shares himself as both a feeling and a thinking person within the structure of two related narratives.[8] In the first, Weatherhead tells of an early morning walk one September morning. The narrative combines description and statement: "The sun was peeping over the horizon, throwing long shadows upon the grass. It was an hour of bewitching loveliness." The descriptions offer Weatherhead to the reader as feeling and responding. The statements present him as thinking, "making sense of," connecting: "I had that strange impression . . . that I was being allowed to be present just as God had concluded the creation of the world. . . ." The same combination of description-response and statement-connection characterizes the second narrative. The description is different and longer and another conclusion is drawn, but Weatherhead becomes increasingly available in the sermon as a feeling and thinking self.

It is the person as willing that does not often appear in sermonic literature, either with or without disclosure of other aspects of self. Weatherhead, for example, ends his narratives in "The Significance of Silence" with a statement of meaning and significance. He does not tell us, however, what difference, if any, was brought about by his experience and his reflection upon it. We do not see him in action beyond the story and we see no projections from the story into other places and other times. If the world looked different to Weatherhead because of the events, and if he acted differently or with new resolve because of what happened, we are not told so. One resulting action, of course, is the sermon itself and the use in it of that which is remembered. But that is action of a different sort; it is not an integral part of the narrative.

One readily available narrative sermon in which there is a more fully disclosed self is Fred B. Craddock's "Doxology."[9] By means of personal story, Craddock creates an image for us and himself of his emotive self. We see him and join him laughing, enjoying, struggling, evading, grieving, and thanking. Craddock also reveals himself as thinker and learner. The question Is Doxology ever out of place? is asked and answered again and again in the negative. Connections are made between diverse incidents and settings: a family supper, a hospital room, a family vacation, a seminary classroom, a small hotel in Austria, a death in the family. Connections are made also between these incidents and the nature of theology: Doxology is most appropriate for the theologian because "theology begins with words not *about* God but *to* God."[10] Craddock has learned something by the end of the sermon and so have we—not only is Doxology never out of place, but "if we ever lose our Doxology we might as well be dead." There is probably no guarantee in the sermon that Craddock will never again be caught without Doxology. He has been caught once too often. Nonetheless we see signs of change, signs of the difference it all makes, within the sermon itself. Perhaps Craddock could not have interpreted as perceptively as he does the cause of cooling zeal, weakening faith, and disappearing appetite among some seminarians apart from the experiences that precede and follow that interpretation in the sermon. Of more significance is the fact that the sermon itself ends in Doxology. What Craddock affirms is acted upon. If we ever lose our Doxology we might as well be dead. So, "from him and through him and to him are all things. To him be glory forever." We both see and hear Craddock enact the meaning and significance of what has been experienced.

Not many months ago I preached a sermon based on Matt. 18:15–20, a passage concerned with church rule and the administration of discipline within the church community. Anyone who has preached on this text knows that it is problematic. Not only are its origins obscure, but the course of action it outlines seems woefully antiquated and unworkable. It seemed important to me to openly admit the latter difficulties. In part, I planned to do so by describing a recent Phil Donahue show in which Matthew 18 was used to justify the actions of a congregation toward a wayward member. Most of the audience agreed with the offending party, who had sued the church. Matthew 18 was literally laughed out of the studio. Someone said, "The church has no right to mess around in one's private life." I planned to express my resentment at such a treatment of Matthew 18, but then admit that I had my own reasons for being wary of the discipline suggested. I would tell the story of the oral examination I underwent prior to my ordination. The church's presiding bishop asked me if I could see sin in other people. How does one answer a question like that? To say no suggests an unseeing, nonthinking dullard; it is an unacceptable response. The question must be answered with a yes, at least if one intends to enact the discipline of Matthew 18. But saying yes paints the unsavory picture of a hawk circling prey. In telling the story I wanted to try to convey my dilemma, my frustration, and my physical and mental discomfort. I longed to avoid the question altogether or to equivocate, but neither was possible. It isn't easy to publicly affirm Matthew 18 and what it implies and assumes.

I also planned to tell the story of the time when I tried to enact Matthew 18 in a parish setting. Without elaborating, let me simply say that it didn't work out very well. In fact, after many months of literally applying the text to the situation, I had to admit that the enactment did not work at all. People, I discovered, do not want to be what the text calls "witnesses," even if they agree that a sin has been committed. I also discovered that offenders can refuse to be excluded just as surely as they can refuse to be reconciled. Again, in telling this story I wanted to try to describe my feelings and my reflections as accurately as possible.

It seemed important to me also, however, to demonstrate what difference, if any, my experience of these events had made. I planned to do this by sharing my renewed determination to locate a viable place for the Matthean passage in congregational life. That may sound pretentious, but I only wanted to do what Ernst Lange claims is the main task of the sermon, that is, to consider the biblical word, to question it, and present what is relevant.[11] I was unwilling to disregard the text, either by ignoring it altogether or by segmenting it. And, because of my experiences, I was unwilling to present the details of the text uncritically. My determination issued in a new, or revitalized, insight. Whatever one does specifically with the Matthean rules of discipline, these rules must be allowed to announce a central fact about the church. The church is a community that lives only under the forgiving mercy of God. What is finally at stake in church discipline is forgiveness. To turn away from occasions of sin, to let one remain in sin, to allow alienation caused by sin to continue—all are refusals to trust the reconciling power of forgiveness. Discipline guards forgiveness.

In the sermon that I finally preached on Matt. 18:15–20, I think that I was able to demonstrate what difference my discovery had made. I shared the development of my insight regarding the connection between discipline and forgiveness. But I also shared my conviction that discipline was more essential to the Christian life than even I as pastor had allowed. And I expressed my resolve that neither widespread moral relativity nor my own unhappy experiences with questions of discipline would keep me from honoring its significance.

In a sense, of course, the demand that the preacher be present as a whole person in shared events of self-portrayal is a demand that is impossible to meet. This is perhaps why it is so difficult to locate sermonic examples that disclose preachers as thinking, feeling, and willing persons. But even when such examples do occur, it would be naive to assume that somehow we are hearing the whole story. Such an assumption would overlook the obvious fact that autobiography is art rather than story. An event shared in story is a selected event and the recounting of it is itself the result of intentional shaping. Such an assumption would also overlook the fact that any person's story is limited. It is limited by "a refusal to face reality, to understand intelligently, to judge reasonably, and to act responsibly."[12] It is limited by "sensibility, inhibitions, language, . . . inclinations to wish, hope, believe, dream."[13] It is limited by blindness to the "part played by money, social class, tradition and ideology."[14] These limitations cannot be avoided by those who desire to tell personal stories of self-portrayal in the pulpit. They are limitations, however, which affect all preachers and all forms of proclamation. One who never tells a personal story faces the same limitations as surely as one who does. And the need for constant self-criticism is a necessity for both. Both need to work at uncovering the limitations of their own viewpoint.

Writers on autobiography are well aware of the possibility of self-deception on the part of the teller. This possibility also challenges the assumption that what we hear in an event of self-portrayal is the whole story. The root of self-deception in telling one's story lies in the "desire to achieve a high degree of consistency and coherence . . . at the expense of comprehensiveness of vision."[15] Self-deception issues in "cover-stories" that protect the teller from having to face certain features of his or her life story. Such "cover-stories" screen out all inconsistencies, all data that do not reinforce the stories told. While such self-deception is always a possibility in personal stories, it need not triumph. Michael Goldberg, for example, has suggested that what is needed by autobiographers is "a story which is expansive and comprehensive enough to allow them to acknowledge and incorporate disharmonious and unflattering elements in their lives."[16] John Shea and others have identified such an expansive and comprehensive story as "the story of God's unconditional acceptance of mankind."[17] Within such a framework the need for falsified stories disappears and the creative urge to know is set loose. In words that we have used already, the preacher who is totally dependent upon the presence, grace, and power of God can afford to be honest.

THE INTERRELATED SELF

According to my understanding of self-portrayal, it is essential that the narrator do more than simply describe his or her experience as a kind of interior moment. The teller of the personal story must try to show the self in its interrelatedness. In part, this means that the narrator must detail the context in which the personal experience occurred. At all points there needs to be a correlation between what is happening within and without. The listener should be able to see and participate in the circumstances that evoke the personal response of the storyteller. We need to know, for example, what brought Martin Luther King, Jr., to the kitchen table in a prayer of surrender. We have to know about the threatening letters and calls, and we have to hear the angry "Listen, nigger" at the end of an exhausting day. Without such details, Dr. King's deeply personal experience will remain an abstraction. Showing the self in its interrelatedness also means that the narrator needs to connect his or her personal experience to the lives of others and to the active presence of God. To do less than this would falsify the self. It would also truncate the tale's possibilities as a vehicle of proclamation. If the tale is to be proclamation, the listener needs to see in what way the personal story is also hers or his. If it is to be proclamation, the listener also needs to know how the now-mutual story relates to the ongoing story of God.

Preached sermons exhibit at least three ways by which the narrator of a personal story can make the necessary connections. The first is by a clear announcement of the narrator's discovery as one that has profound significance for the listener. Fred Craddock, for example, announces the significance that his discovery has beyond his own life. He concludes that nothing is more appropriate than Doxology "for any of us, whoever or wherever or however."[18] That conclusion has been won on behalf of all his listeners, and it is offered to them as a possible conclusion for the living of their own lives. The discovery is a bridge between speaker and listener. It is a discovery that touches the nerve center of St. Paul's burst of praise in Rom. 11:33–36. It is supported by the credibility of Craddock's personal story. It announces a profound and general truth of life that cannot only be thought about, but can be put into immediate use. Martin Luther King, Jr., concludes with Jude 24 that "God is able to give us the interior resources to face the storms and problems of life."[19] This conclusion is his own but it is also a conclusion won for, and offered to, his listeners. It is a credible conclusion because, like Craddock's, it follows naturally from his experience. It is credible also because it withstands a harsh subsequent test. The truth of God's ability to provide inner resources is further demonstrated when King's home is bombed and he is able to accept the word of the bombing calmly. God is able to provide an inner calm that is good for both internal and external turmoil. King tells his audience that what he discovered is exactly what they all need. "It will give us courage. . . . It will give our tired feet new strength. . . . This is our hope for becoming better men . . . our mandate for seeking to make a better world."[20]

Narrators of personal story connect with others in a second way by making certain that the story told touches the "level of existential feelings, of expectation, disappointment, yearning, joy, sadness, and desire" that all people share.[21] Hans van der Geest is right when he claims that this touching of existential feelings is more important than a similarity of situations. "Fathers and mothers without children," he asserts, "can also participate in the experience of motherly fear and relief."[22] Because everyone knows a yearning for freedom, a story about imprisonment can speak to those who have never been behind bars.

I, like John Claypool, have had close friends ask me if God really helps a person in time of trouble. Unlike John Claypool, however, I have not had that question raised by a friend at the very time a young daughter was dying of acute leukemia. Nor have I had that question asked by a dying daughter in terms of a cure, "Have you asked God when it will go away? What did he say?"[23] All of which is to say that the situation described so movingly by John Claypool in his sermon "To Walk and Not to Faint" has never been mine. I have never been where he was. I have not stood beside a hospital bed watching pain rack every part of my daughter's body. I have never faced a time when "the heavens seemed utterly silent and even locked from the inside." And I have never had a friend ask me in the midst of heaven's silence, "When the chips are really down, does this 'thing' we call God really make any difference?"[24]

The story John Claypool tells is deeply personal. Yet it is also my story. Not because of the situation it relates, but because it touches the level of existential feeling. I know what it is to feel helpless before a questioner. I know what it is to hope against hope for that which has no chance of coming to pass. I know what it is to watch someone I love suffer a deprivation that seems without meaning. Claypool's story is both his and mine at the level of existential feeling, and I listen intensely as he honestly searches for an answer. What Claypool discovered in his experience was the third part of Isaiah's promise in Isa. 40:31: the promise of the gift of endurance. Claypool found no ecstasy (no "mounting up with wings like eagles"). He found no conclusive answers (no "running and not being weary"). What he found was the strength to "walk and not faint." By the grace of God, he says, "Somehow I stayed on my feet. . . . I was given the gift just to stand and hold on."[25] And that becomes Claypool's answer to himself, his friend, and to us. "I can say out of honest experience. . . . You may not be able to soar or even to run, but to walk and not faint—*it will be given!*"[26] That affirmation becomes a real answer and promise to me because Claypool's story is also mine.

A sermon by John R. Fry exhibits yet another way of connecting the preacher's story with those of his or her listeners.[27] In "Deafness," Fry tells what it was like for him to be mute for six days following an injury to his mouth during a football game. He begins by describing the effect of the muteness on himself and on his friends and family. He writes, "I could listen, but could not join"; "I was only a watcher of the action"; "My inability to talk had cut some deep nerve."[28] "People began speaking for me," he also writes. Because "I could not talk even in that short period, my friends and family, it seemed, almost acted as though I could not hear either."[29] Fry connects these observations with a social world in which many people are inarticulate. "You don't have any say," he insists. "You cannot protest. You cannot affirm. You cannot question. You cannot answer questions."[30] Thus he speaks for the functioning mute as well as the congenital mute: the Third World, the politically voiceless, the autistic, the angry. Fry then makes one final connection. We are dealing, he says, "with muteness far beyond all political social constructions"; "Muteness is a pre-figuring of death from where no sound emerges."[31] John Fry's six-day football injury has become the source of an ever-expanding exploration of muteness. He extends the context; he gives muteness a voice and it speaks of a personal, social, and cosmic phenomenon. The text for the sermon is Matt. 9:27–34; the story of a dumb man whose demon was driven out by Jesus. Fry sees in this action of Jesus a mandate for the Christian congregation. They are to exorcise the demons that make people dumb, ridding them of the fear of death and giving them back their voice. "The end of exorcism is sound: *creative sound*," he writes. "Human speech from the no longer voiceless."[32]

At this point I want to suggest that personal stories honoring the interrelated self can escape the accusation of privatism. Most preachers I have talked to about personal story express a fear of the idiosyncratic. Many seem to assume that any personal story is doomed from the outset to monadic expression. I hope that I have been able to demonstrate that such need not be the case. At least three bridges between the narrating self and others can be built deftly and securely. One can connect by announcing his or her discovery, by narrating at the level of existential feelings, or by extending the personal into the social and cosmic. And in each case the connection is not simply between personal story and others but also between personal story and the presence and activity of God. Failure to build these bridges is not a failure of personal story. It is rather a failure of the narrator in intention and skill.

4
Self-Portrayal and
the Biblical Text

Many fear the uncontrolled use of personal story in pulpit preaching. Their fear is not unwarranted. All too frequently, a personal story is told that suggests no reason for its telling other than the fact that it happened to the teller. It seems unattached to anything other than to the one who speaks. It leaves the impression that the preacher needs to fill time, or needs to tell the story for his or her own sake alone. It should be clear that this book is not encouraging such unattached, time-filler stories of self-expression. Nonetheless, it is important to restate and enlarge upon some essential matters that were touched upon earlier.

While I have encouraged preachers to share their experiences from the pulpit, it is not their experiences per se that I have encouraged them to share. It is their experiences of the good news that I have urged them to narrate. While I have encouraged preachers to offer their opinions from the pulpit, it is not their opinions per se that I have encouraged them to offer. It is their opinions about the relevance of the transmitted tradition that I have urged them to speak. While I have encouraged preachers to tell about the events of their lives, it is not the events per se that I have encouraged them to relate. It is of events connected to the Word that I have urged them to tell. The story of the preacher must always be attached to the good news, the transmitted tradition, the Word. Only in this way can the preacher's story become a vehicle for the Word of God. Only in this way can the events of the preacher's life serve "the prismatic function of catching the gospel's rays."

Gustaf Wingren is right in the advice he gives the preacher who intends to share personal experience with a congregation. Two things, Wingren says, should be kept in mind as a "protection": "the aim, *scopus*—that Christ may come through the word; and simplicity, *simplicitas*—that the actual text of the passage must determine what is said."[1] The preacher needs this protection, Wingren insists, because our ability to speculate is too great. We are always in danger either of casting the passage aside altogether or of using the passage only as an excuse for pursuing side issues. But the congregation needs this protection also. If the text is cast aside, if voice is not given to the Word, then "life does not come to the listener."[2] This is the case because God's "creative Word speaks to us out of every Biblical passage" and because preaching "possesses, as a continuation of the Bible . . . the same might which once created the world, and shall one day create the world anew."[3] That is, a preacher's personal story participates in the life-giving power of the creative Word when it is subject to the biblical text. This subjection, it might be noted, safeguards all proclamation. It is a necessity for all preaching, regardless of the form it takes.

It is significant that Wingren does not separate *simplicitas* and *scopus*. The actual text of the passage cannot be separated from the aim of all preaching. There is a stream, Wingren insists, that flows deep down in every individual passage. It is the stream of Christ's death and resurrection.[4] This is the center of the news about Christ. This news about Christ is the center of the New Testament,[5] and it is toward this news that all in the Bible tends.[6] By such an emphasis on *scopus*, Wingren necessitates a place for theology in preaching as well as a place for the individual text. Theology cannot help but serve as a mediator between text and preacher. Each particular text raises the question of its relation to the "core of faith," to the "news about Christ."[7] The question is raised as soon as preachers try to make theological sense out of a text that makes an array of affirmations all at the same time. As Richard Lischer asks: "How *does* one map a way through providence, election, predestination, justification, and resurrection in Rom. 8:28–30?"[8] The question is also raised as soon as preachers try to articulate the implications that the "news about Christ" has for daily life. As Elizabeth Achtemeier asks, "But what does it mean to be 'saved' as we pursue our common, everyday rounds of work? Or what *is* the new meaning given by Jesus Christ to my ordinary life as a housewife and mother?"[9] Questions like these cannot be sidetracked. Preachers using personal story cannot avoid them. Their stories must be subject to the individual text and to the "news about Christ." Their stories must point to the center, and they must point to the significance of that center for those who listen.

Preachers who have used personal story in their sermons exhibit varying degrees of subjection to biblical texts. On occasion, some have used no text whatsoever, or they have ignored the text so completely that it has all but disappeared. Such a minimal degree of subjection, however, does not distinguish preachers who use personal story from preachers who do not. Texts have a way of remaining invisible or of evaporating in all kinds of sermons. Preachers who come nowhere near using narratives of self-portrayal can dismiss the text as easily as the most avid storytellers.

Even when the individual text is clearly present, it is possible for tellers of personal story to trivialize the text. This happens when the related event is one that did not capture the narrator, that involved no discovery, or that is incapable of bearing connections. This is what seems to happen, for example, in Helmut Thielicke's otherwise splendid sermon, "The Parable of the Wise and Foolish Maidens."[10] Thielicke describes the wise maidens in Jesus' story as "people who live by the faithfulness of this One Man," Jesus Christ.[11] He wants to emphasize the fact that when a person looks at this One Man "the strange and alien becomes familiar" and when one looks away from him "our ship becomes an uncanny, alien place, drifting in a void." Thielicke's lead into this summary is in part his experience of observing two dogs on a ship voyage to and from America. One dog, separated from his owner, was condemned, Thielicke says, "to a creaturely form of nihilism": his "whole familiar dog world had come to an end. . . . Beyond was only enemy country." The second dog had his young mistress with him. He too, Thielicke writes, "missed the familiar streets and did not know what was wrong with this strange world." But when this dog looked at his owner, with a "look of animal trust," he was reassured; he knew that the sensible world would return once again. "Not only out of the mouths of babes," Thielicke concludes, "but also from the eyes of dogs, can God bring perfect praise." This brief incident is inadequate insofar as it fails to include essential elements of self-portrayal. Thielicke is not present as a whole person. We do not know exactly how he feels about the incident, nor what real difference it makes to him. (One cannot help but wonder why he is so observant of the dogs on board when there were probably people on board exhibiting the same degree of estrangement and trust.) Again, there is no indication that Thielicke discovered anything. We are left feeling that Thielicke already knew that "from the eyes of dogs, can God bring perfect praise." This brief incident is also inadequate in its connecting story with text and aim, with both *simplicitas* and *scopus*. The trusting dog is simply not the equivalent of the wise maidens, nor is it the equivalent of the Christian believer who depends on the One Man for all things. The reader is left thinking far more about dogs than about Jesus' story or the one who tells it. If Thielicke had been able to share a personal discovery and its effect upon him, the dog story might have been integral in putting the reader back into the text and into the presence of the One Man. But the story and Thielicke's observations cannot do it alone. The story simply does not represent the text or Thielicke's aim satisfactorily.

Trivialization of the text is one error into which tellers of personal story can fall. Another is what I call parallelism. This happens when the text and the personal story parallel one another, but fail to come together and inform each other. An example of this parallelism can be found in Leslie Weatherhead's sermon "The Significance of Silence." Weatherhead tells of an experience of silence while on an early walk in a meadow, and of an experience when the sound of a train and the sound of a village clock interpreted the silence of a farm at midnight. Of the second experience he concludes: "Sounds of that nature interpret the silence, they alone making one apprehend how utterly still and quiet is the night."[12] Immediately after the second story Weatherhead writes, "I felt that I understood a little better that strange experience of Elijah" (1 Kings 19:12). Then he quickly moves on to consider "how often the hour of the soul's exaltation is an hour of silence." Weatherhead's experience sounds roughly similar to that of Elijah, inasmuch as silence in each case received an interpreting sound. Beyond that apparent similarity, however, there is no informing connection between the two. Was the only significance of the "still small voice" for Elijah to be found in the fact that now he apprehended how "utterly still and quiet is the night"? Or perhaps only that Elijah now knew that God had brought him to "that hour and to that place"? But what was the content of the silence that followed wind, earthquake, and fire? What were the sounds made by the "Lord, the God of hosts"? These questions seem to lie at the heart of the biblical text. They receive no hearing and certainly no answers from Weatherhead's personal narrative. Personal story and text touch, but they do not meet. And because they do not meet, the "news about Christ," toward which all in the Bible tends, is muffled. A simple parallel between text and personal story is inadequate as proclamation.

Certainly the biblical text is not always forgotten, trivialized, or only paralleled by preachers who use personal story in their sermons. There are many instances when the text has come alive through its association with narratives of self-portrayal. A sermon by D. W. Cleverley Ford demonstrates one way by which a healthy linkage can be accomplished. The sermon is entitled "When Preaching Is Effective" and is based on Acts 13:42: "And as they went out, they besought that these words might be spoken to them the next sabbath" (ASV).[13] Ford is convinced by the people of Antioch and by his own experience that if a preacher appeals to human need, people will go and hear him or her "next Sunday, and the Sunday after." He recalls an incident when he was a student, "straying from my own religious denomination," "perhaps overworking," frightened by "the examination" looming ahead. In a condition of great need he went to City Temple one Sunday and sat "rooted to the pew" during a sermon preached by a layman, a lecturer in ancient history at the University of Cambridge. He was "an ugly man in an ugly church," Ford writes, "but the grace of God was on his lips." The layman spoke of God's strengthening power in time of temptation, and Ford "gained the stiffening he so eloquently talked about." "I returned there the next Sunday," Ford says, "to hear those words again." The event in Antioch and the event in City Temple do more than parallel one another. Both take place in worship, both involve hearing the good news and both express an urgent longing for the occasion to occur again. (The RSV translates Acts 13:42, "The people begged that these things might be told them the next sabbath.") Ford's narrative assists his listeners in tapping the energy behind the "begging" of the "men of Israel." In a sense, Ford's experience authenticating the account of Acts 13:42 and the event in Antioch adds significance to Ford's experience in City Temple. Ford's encounter was not an isolated one, an experience without precedent. The encounter recurs each time the word of grace is spoken and heard.

The personal story told by Cleverley Ford provides a contemporary equivalent of the biblical story. This is one way in which a particular text can be honored, as well as the God whose Word finds normative literary articulation in the text. A second means for connecting text and personal story is suggested by John Claypool's sermon "Strength Not to Faint."[14] Elements of this sermon are quite similar to another of Claypool's which was used as an example of a story that touches the level of existential feeling.[15] "Strength Not to Faint" demonstrates how a personal story can aid in understanding a biblical text by being interwoven with it. Claypool's text is again Isa. 40:27–31. Over against the three forms of God's promised strength in these verses, Claypool places the experience of standing by his intensely suffering and dying daughter Laura Lue. God's strength can take the form of ecstasy ("to mount up with wings as eagles"), he says, but when "standing by a bed with a little child moaning and thinking the night would never end—ecstasy is not only inappropriate, it is downright impossible. . . ." God's help is also described in Isaiah as strength for activism, but for Claypool there "was simply no room 'to run and not be weary' "; there was no way "to attack this problem by force, no solution of activism or energy." Fortunately, Claypool writes, there is one other form that the promise of God's strength takes: "They shall walk and not faint." What is promised may not sound like much of a religious experience, he admits, but "when there is no occasion to soar and no place to run, and all you can do is trudge along step by step, to hear of a Help that will enable you 'to walk and not faint' is good news indeed." Claypool concludes not only that the Isaiah text is supremely accurate, but that it has put the promises of God in ascending order. The most difficult discipline is not that of soaring or even of running. It consists, he says, in keeping on "when it seems that in spite of everything you are going to crumble under the load and faint away." In this sermon Claypool tries the verity of biblical text; he measures it against his own experience of God's strength. He does not find the promises of God wanting, but he does insist that not all of God's promises ought to be expected in any one situation. The harsh realities of his own story have issued in a "realization . . . of crucial importance" and thus saved him from false expectations. The encounter between story and promise has clarified the biblical message and has made it immediately accessible to

Claypool's listeners. Reflecting on Claypool's story, listeners will probably remember the promises of "good news" in Isaiah; reflecting upon
the Isaiah text, listeners will probably remember Claypool's story and
his "realization of crucial importance." Text and story have been woven
together, and the story helps us make sense of the text.

Claypool's story of how he was able to face his daughter's suffering
and death opens ears to hearing Isaiah 40 in a new way. Obviously,
not all personal stories are of such momentous proportions. Smaller
stories may not be sizable enough to be thoroughly interwoven with
a strategic biblical passage. Even stories of smaller proportions, however, can ready listeners to hear the text and the good news of Christ.
Leslie Weatherhead, for example, uses a personal narrative to ready
ears for a hearing of John 14:13, "Whatsoever ye shall ask in my name,
that will I do" (KJV). Weatherhead begins starkly, not by asking what
the words of this promise mean, but by asking whether they mean
anything at all. He raises this question in all seriousness, recalling an
incident in which he "lost a good deal of faith" as a boy of fifteen.[16]
Facing an examination that he "very badly wanted to pass," Weatherhead reminded God in prayer that Christ had promised "that whatsoever we asked in his name we should have." The words of the promise
seemed "definite and apparently unambiguous." Weatherhead had
studied hard. He had had "a religious upbringing." Everything seemed
to be going for him. But then he failed! "The lamp flickered that time,"
he writes. "The light almost went out." Weatherhead says he learned
something from the failure. The next year he worked harder and
passed. "Then, I told God I could do without his promises. I could do
things by myself," he writes. Both the personal story and what Weatherhead learned raise significant queries about a familiar text. The listener is quite ready for Weatherhead's offer: "What, then, are we to
make of these words?"

Although Weatherhead's smaller story raises questions about the biblical text in a provocative manner, it is unable to interpret the text
except in a negative way. (Whatever the promise of the text refers to,
it probably does not focus on passing school examinations.) Some smaller stories, however, do provide access to a clear message from the text.
Not long ago I preached a sermon based on Matt. 11:25–30, Jesus'
invitation to "all who labor and are heavy laden."[17] My study of the
text raised a crucial question for me that I felt I had to answer. Why

does the promise of rest in Matthew 11 have to be coupled with bearing a yoke? Why couldn't Jesus simply say, I will take from you all burdens and all causes of burden? Why couldn't he, or didn't he, say that? In the midst of my study I received a long-distance phone call from a close friend. It was good to hear from him, but the conversation was not pleasant. My friend told me that his life was crumbling around him. He was afraid of losing his job and his family. He could not eat, and sleep came only in fitful dozes. An hour or so into the conversation, he let out a deep sigh. "I feel better now," he said. Hours after I hung up the phone I was still thinking about that conversation. Most of all, however, I was thinking about the sigh and the sound of a hard-won rest. The man's problems were still there. Not only had I not erased them, but I had been incapable of giving any sage advice or answers. Yet when we said good-bye, he said, "I think I can sleep now . . . I think I can rest." It suddenly occurred to me that the reason my friend could now rest was because he had let some of his burden go; his yoke had been planed by sharing some of the weight on his back. I learned all over again that when two people share a burden so that one of them can walk a little lighter, it is the work of Jesus. The lifting of weights is not simply something that Jesus wants done, but it is the work of Jesus himself. It also occurred to me that the reason I had been feeling restful myself since the end of the conversation was because during the conversation I had been wearing the yoke of Jesus. Without my conscious awareness I had been used in Jesus' own work of giving rest. I learned all over again that whenever we do what we are supposed to do as followers of Jesus, the burden *is* light and the yoke *is* easy. Whenever we share in God's work of lifting and healing, our lives are full of meaning and purpose, and that makes for rest.

To be sure, the interpretation of Matt. 11:25–30 to which I was opened by my personal experience is not the only possible interpretation of these verses. It is an indication, however, that even a story of small proportions can yield insights into texts to which they have affinity. Such a story may only provide the experiential context out of which a text is questioned, as in the case of Weatherhead's sermon. Such a story, however, may also provide access to answers within the text to questions that an encounter with the text itself raises. Personal stories both small and large can thus aid us in understanding the biblical texts and the "good news of Christ." And they can speak those understandings and good news to listeners at the level of their experience and interest. I was surprised, for example, by the number and intensity of conversations that followed the preaching of my sermon on Matthew 11. Many claimed that they had been led to think about rest and yoke bearing in a new way. Many others claimed that they themselves now felt at rest.

Personal story can also enable preachers to enter the text and see both it and themselves from the inside. Here it is not a matter of raising questions or of answering them. It is a matter of identifying with someone in the text and allowing that identification to run its course. This is not quite the same as providing a contemporary equivalent of a situation, or even of a person, in the text. It is an identification that leads where it will. An example of such identifying can be found in Helmut Thielicke's sermon "The Parable of the Tares among the Wheat."[18] In this sermon Thielicke becomes one of the servants in Matt. 13:24–30 who wants to go and rid the householder's field of an enemy's weeds. The personal story he shares identifies him as one ready to organize a great "Operation Throw-them-out." It also identifies him as one who hears the householder's final words: "Let both grow until the harvest." Thielicke tells of his visit to the United Nations in New York and of his "terrible anger" at viewing the Meditation Room, "a temple of utterly weird desolation, an empty, ruined field of a faith long since fled." All of the conference rooms, he says, were furnished with the utmost in comfort; "everything had been thought of, nothing was missing." Only in the meditation room, "where the ultimate was at stake, only here was emptiness and desolation." Later Thielicke grew ashamed of his anger, which he had expressed "somewhat rashly" and which was "not unlike that of the servants in the parable." He began to wonder whether the "small, very forlorn, very timid" room was perhaps a sign that somebody knew that the fate of nations is not simply a matter of political debate, strategy, and diplomacy. He began to question who was capable enough to separate the nihilistic element in the worship room from "the seed of a true knowledge which may yet spring up here, from the spiritual poverty which here awaits its promise." In his anger, Thielicke has become one of the parable's servants. By the end of the story he has become a servant taught. He has heard the words of the householder: "Let both grow until the harvest."

Such a confluence of personal story and text/aim as is suggested here certainly aids the preacher in dealing with what George W. Stroup, III, has identified as two of the "perennial questions": "What does theology have to do with experience?" and "How does a historical document such as the Bible speak to contemporary men and women?"[19]

It can be claimed that the whole attempt to bring story and the inherited tradition together in recent times is a bid to make theological reflection an integral component of the life process. I claim that this is exactly what happens in the sermonic flowing together of personal story and text/aim. Such preaching can lead people to a faith-appropriation of their experiences. It can help them "clearly articulate the religious, theological, and ecclesiological dimensions of their situation."[20] Such preaching enables the preacher to be a theological resource, relating situations to Christian understandings and values.

Such a confluence of personal story and text/aim also places the preacher's personal story clearly where it belongs. Elie Wiesel rightly insists that storytellers do not begin their stories with their own story. Each storyteller's tale is "fitted into the memory that is the living tradition of his people."[21] The preacher's own story never stands alone. It does not initiate itself, nor does it conclude itself. It is always a story within a Christian story. This Christian story includes the biblical narratives. But it also includes "the history of their appropriation by previous Christian communities and the interpretation of that tradition in the present."[22] The preacher's tale is always and only a part of this living tradition.

5
Self-Portrayal
and the Sermon

The personal stories used as examples in this book are clearly of different kinds. They differ in subject matter. Childhood, family, school, ministry, travel, friends, war, birth, death—these and more are deemed apt material for reflection and sharing. The stories differ in intensity. Some are told about singular and formative events in the teller's life, while others are told about happenings more or less common to all. The stories also differ in length. None of the stories referred to in this book constitute an entire sermon. They are interwoven with other stories, including that of the biblical text, and they are interpreted. Some are two to three pages long, while others are a brief paragraph in length. And just as the stories differ, so do the preachers. They differ in the degree to which they use personal story in their sermons. Any impression that all of them use personal stories in each and every sermon should be corrected. Some use first-person singular narrative most sparingly. Indeed, there are only a few who detail their own lives with any regularity. These preachers also differ in the manner of their telling. Some provide far more details than others in describing settings or characters. Some include more dialogue than others, allowing the reader to hear the characters speak for themselves.

The sheer variety of personal stories should relax those preachers who feel that they have no stories to share, or who wonder if there will be any stories left after six months. The preacher who asks, What do I share after I've told the one or two major events of my life? has missed the point. Not every personal story need be singular. In fact, to tell of only the most memorable events may imply a falsehood. It may imply that God is at work only in the extraordinary occurrences of our lives and not in the commonplace.[1] It is certainly true, however, that the significance of the commonplace can often elude us. "I wish things like that would happen to me," preachers frequently say after they have heard another's story. But the fact is that "things like that" do happen to all of us. What we need to do is pay more attention to them. Things happen all the time that make us laugh or cry. We see people and situations every day that make our stomachs knot or that free us from ourselves and our tasks for even a few moments. We hear sounds that jangle our nerves or that soothingly settle us. Any event that evokes an emotional response from us is a personal story in embryo. It is worth retelling and exploring.

We can work at developing more awareness of the stories in our lives in several ways. One is by reading the autobiographies of some contemporary Christians like Frederick Buechner, Madeleine L'Engle, and David H. C. Read.[2] Another is by working through available material on writing one's own story.[3] Still another is by keeping a journal for fifteen or twenty minutes a day that focuses on people or events that evoked a strong emotional response.[4]

The varying length and differing styles of the personal stories should encourage experimentation and relax preachers who fear that there is only one way of doing this type of narrative. The personal story does not always have to begin the sermon, nor end it. It can be told in the middle of the sermon or at any other point. Stories need not be told always in the same style. Some can emphasize setting, while others can focus on character. Some stories may be given an interpretation. Others may be left open-ended with only clues pointing toward a conclusion. Most of us know what we like in a story and therefore have some idea of what constitutes a good telling. With practice we can begin to match our own storytelling with the standards we apply to the storytelling of others. Reading stories told by other preachers can help. So can reading short stories and novels. Books on storytelling and on the craft of story writing may also prove to be invaluable aids.[5]

Personal stories of self-portrayal used in sermons can and should assume a variety of lengths, shapes, and styles. These differences are relatively unimportant. They are unimportant in comparison with certain essentials which have already been elaborated. The preacher's story should have a revelatory dimension, a shared discovery. It should show the teller in the fullness of her or his personhood and in a social-cultural context. The story must be inseparably attached to the good news and be subject to the biblical text. To these necessities there must now be added another. The personal story must be thoroughly integrated with the rest of the sermon.

The full potential of autobiographical narrative is reached only when the narrative is an integral part of the sermon in which it appears. The validity of such a claim seems obvious, but there is a difference between acknowledging that integration is necessary and making it happen. Published preachers who use the narrative form of self-portrayal often fall into familiar traps short of the desired goal. To look at some of their failures is certainly not to suggest their inadequacy in sharing a personal story. It is rather to suggest that their lapses can be instructive. The point at which even the best have difficulty is a good place to pay close attention. It also suggests that there are none of us who do not need to learn more about his or her art.

Sometimes a good preacher seems to use a personal narrative just because he or she wants to. Its focus is not all that significant and there are no clear lines drawn from it, or by it, to what follows or by what precedes. In his sermon "Did Jesus Really Still a Storm?" for example, Leslie Weatherhead tells of a trip across the Sea of Galilee in the summer of 1934.[6] Having laughed at the boatman's warning of a sudden storm, Weatherhead and his friends nonetheless started for home earlier than they wanted. Within a few moments a storm arose that whipped the water into threatening waves, "and an hour or so afterward," he writes, "drenched to the skin with spray, wiser and sadder men and women, we disembarked." He continues, "Yet before we had finished lunch, the lake looked as calm and innocent again as when we had set out." After providing a brief explanation of the cause of such sudden storms, Weatherhead adds corroborating testimony from Basil Matthews's *The Life of Jesus,* and from George Adam Smith's *Historical Geography of the Holy Land.* He then raises a question about the Markan account, which attributes the sudden cessation of a Galilean storm to the words of Jesus. "What are we to make of the certain fact that sudden cessations . . . took place before Jesus' life and have taken place since . . .?"[7] Weatherhead's story is typically well told, but it

appears to be unnecessary. Three witnesses to the same natural phenomenon, especially one already made familiar (in a footnote Weatherhead refers to four additional authors and books), seems like an ex-
travagance.

If Weatherhead felt that there had to be three, he could have added
his own witness without telling the story. Indeed, the story gets in the
way. The narrative's details are so vivid, and the natural explanation
so interesting, that the reader is caught up in the phenomenal Sea of
Galilee. The rather abrupt transition to St. Mark's account comes as
an interruption. The story focuses attention on the sea and not on the
tension between natural and supernatural causation. The narrative is
interesting but it is more of an excursion than it is a direct path.

There are times when preachers seem to have misread the personal
stories they tell—the narratives they share seem to say something other
than what the narrators say they do. Whatever integration follows,
therefore, is a bit askew. In his sermon "The More Excellent Way," D.
W. Cleverley Ford needs an example of an effective preacher, scholar,
or administrator who "has love."[8] He tells of inviting "one of the most
able men in the Church of England" to preach in his struggling first
church. The man did not come, but "he wrote such a kindly refusal,
conveying such a spirit of humility and graciousness. . . . I have paid
attention to him ever since." There is certainly no reason to doubt the
truth of what Ford says. But what he says is more his private reaction
than it is a fact demonstrated by the narrative. The written refusal is
not read (it was written on a post card!). Why Ford felt that his invitation
was such a "daring thing" we are not told. Again, Ford is certainly not
lying, but the simple narrative does not verify his interpretation. And
because there is no narrative verification, the existence of a loving
preacher, scholar, or administrator is not proved. Ford might just as
well have insisted that such people do exist and let it go at that.

Another brief first-person narrative that allows a different interpretation than the preacher gives it is found in Helmut Thielicke's "The
Parable of the Tares Among the Wheat."[9] Thielicke quotes an attender
at St. Michael's who said, "All this fuss that's going on about the preaching in St. Michael's has nothing whatsoever to do with spiritual fruit;
it's pure sensation seeking, almost a fad. The people come to get a
thrill or see what's going on, but certainly not to attend worship."[10]

Thielicke fairly states that the man who said these things did not suggest, like the servants in the parable, that the "weed patch" at St. Michael's should be exterminated. "Nevertheless," Thielicke says, "he did intimate that what was flourishing here was some kind of weed anyhow." But what are the weeds? In what he says, Thielicke assumes that they are the people who are felt to lack spiritual sincerity, and he continues the sermon on that basis. But what if the accusing man felt that the weeds were Thielicke's sermons? His accusation focuses as much on the preaching at St. Michael's as it does on those who seek a thrill. The integration of Thielicke's sermons as the weeds in need of extermination would require a far different sermonic development than the one that occurs. Because Thielicke's story is open to an interpretation that he does not admit, there is an integrative strain.

Sometimes the full potential of an autobiographical narrative is not reached in a sermon because the story is not carried as far as it could go. An initial tale is told, it is given a summary interpretation, and then it is forgotten. It is never referred to again, even though reflection on it would reinforce and make vivid the sermon's developing theme. It is not integrated and it is therefore partially wasted. In another sermon on the parables, Thielicke recalls his first Bible-study hour as a pastor. [11] Hitler was "in the saddle, and his dreadful power machine were merely puppets hanging by strings in the hands of this mighty Lord." Determined, however, to trust Jesus' saying, "All power is given unto me in heaven and earth," Thielicke entered the room and was met by an audience of three. In contrast to the battalions of youth marching outside, there were inside only "two very old ladies and a still older organist" whose palsied fingers were "embarrassingly apparent in his playing." "So this was the extent of the accomplishment of this Lord, to whom all power in heaven and earth had been given, *supposedly* given." If this is all he has to offer, Thielicke wonders, is he not refuted by "this utterly miserable response?"

Thielicke answers his own question in what follows, but unfortunately makes no further reference to the three old people gathered to study the Bible. They would serve well as a reality factor over against his conclusions. He claims, for example, that the emphasis of the parable of the Mustard Seed (Matt. 13:31–32) is not upon external growth, and bigness, but upon the growth of a Christian's functioning. But if this is true, who then are the three? Are they simply a structural means

of introducing the problem, or are they in some sense a living illustration of the parable's emphasis? Again, Thielicke later draws an important distinction between Christians or the church, and the kingdom
of God. The parable does not mean, he insists, that it is Christendom
or the church or the Christian West that will grow; the parable refers
rather to the growth into Jesus, as his Word is formed in the believer.
But if this is true, did Thielicke perhaps misread the small group gathered for study? Numbers, age, and physical condition are not the most
important things, and certainly they are not a measure of the truth.
Thielicke's words imply such about the three but he never says so. In
a sermon aimed at giving encouragement, the assurances given would
be more substantial if they were applied directly to the dramatic image
of the young pastor and his seemingly inconsequential flock. There,
too, we might also know from where our preacher draws his own encouragement; from the promise of the small and hidden, or from the
numbers that first heard this sermon? It is only at the beginning that
we are told Thielicke's reaction to his congregation of three. Whether
or not the parable's emphasis on smallness and on kingdom finally
enabled him to see in the three something he did not see before is left
open to question.

Integration occurs when the personal story informs the rest of the
sermon of which it is a part. It also occurs when the autobiographical
narrative is itself informed by the sermon's developing themes. In both
cases the narrative is allowed to expand, to probe and be probed. It
is carried forward as far as it will go. There are times, however, when
the narrative cannot be carried forward because the narrative and the
developing theme of the sermon finally tell a different story. They
cannot inform each other because they speak of different things. In
such cases, full integration obviously does not occur. And it is not so
much a matter of the story being stopped before reaching its full potential. It is more a matter of the sermon's potential not being realized
through the narrative.

Reference has been made already to the story told by Theodore
Ferris involving a change in his sermon delivery and the discovery that
empowered that change.[12] The incident nicely demonstrates the essential component of discovery in autobiographical narrative. It also
provides an example of poor integration. Ferris's sermon is addressed
to people who are "likely to assume too much responsibility to care

too much." His own story exhibits how one can care about something "not worth caring about" and how such care can detract from one's "total usefulness." It also illustrates the fact that one can let go of burdensome responsibility and find relief from unnecessary anxiety. Ferris's way of finding relief, however, seems different from the way he suggests to his audience. Once he realized that he was carrying on a fear-producing ritual chiefly for his own satisfaction, Ferris said to himself: "Now I am caring about something that is not worth caring about. . . ." The relief that followed seems dependent on Ferris's act of will, something like saying, This is stupid and I'm simply not going to do it anymore. But by the time Ferris addresses his congregation, he is talking about prayer and is recommending a form that might be used by responsibility-burdened people. "Say something like this," he writes, and then adds, "as we pray that prayer sincerely, the anxiety for those things will be shed." The difference between the methods of relief may seem slighter than it really is. The cause of the burden, the realization of the need, the effect of the relief, all seem similar. But an act of will, which sounds exactly like another responsibility, is different from an act of prayer. Prayer, as Ferris describes its context, is more like an act of surrender: "There are some things that God cares about and takes care of, and . . . we do not need to worry or be concerned about them one way or the other." Perhaps what Ferris said to himself was a prayer. It does not sound like it, however, and the lack of integration causes confusion.

An example of how a personal story can be integrated into the rest of a sermon is found in John Vannorsdall's "The Bus."[13] The sermon begins with the story of Vannorsdall's bus ride from the New Haven train station to the New Haven Green. (See appendix 3 for the text on which the following discussion is based.) "Two young boys who needed transfers had already dropped their money through the slot before they discovered that the driver had no transfers." The driver could not retrieve the coins and the boys had no money left with which to board the next bus. One passenger noted that another bus had pulled up behind them, and the driver suggested that the boys get on it and tell that bus driver that they had already paid their fares. Another passenger spoke for several when he insisted that the driver of the second bus would never believe the boys. The driver of Vannorsdall's bus knew that she should not leave her vehicle for any reason. Encouraged by nonverbal signals from her passengers, however, she got off, walked to the other bus, got two transfers, returned, and gave the transfers to the boys. As Vannorsdall's bus finally departed, the woman next to him shouted across the aisle, "She's new, but she's gonna do all right."

This story of the bus ride seems almost too commonplace to serve as anchor for a sermon on peace. But Vannorsdall makes it work. The rest of the sermon is a reflection on the ride, as well as on the text (John 10:11–16) and the potentially imminent British invasion of the Falkland/Malvina Islands held by Argentine troops (May 1982). Vannorsdall claims that he learned two things on the bus. One is the fact that the other passengers were very knowledgeable about buses. While stating that knowledge is of different kinds and is ubiquitous, Vannorsdall never loses sight of the bus and its passengers. Among other things, he claims that knowledge is "how to get a bus to stop" and knowledge "facilitates a bus ride." But truth is more important than knowledge, Vannorsdall says, and he shares his second lesson from the bus ride. "The people there *cared* about what happened. . . . Their knowledge of buses was not *the* truth, but their knowledge was placed in the service of truth, and truth was in their caring."[14] Knowledge is not redemptive, Vannorsdall asserts. Knowledge makes the buses run, but it is truth that makes human beings human. Truth reaches out to two small boys, it suggests transfers, it encourages a new driver. The sermon ends with the affirmation, "Truth is in buses."

Much of what Vannorsdall says about knowledge and truth, about the good shepherd of John 10, and about the situation in the South Atlantic, has been omitted from this brief summary. But the focus is on integration and the description has emphasized the way in which the personal story has been integrated into the whole. It is the source of the two central lessons advanced by the sermon. Every assertion about knowledge and truth makes use of the bus ride for development, depiction, or both. The bus, the situation, the two boys, the passengers, and the driver are never forgotten. There is reference to one or more of them in almost every paragraph. The sermon begins with the bus and it ends with the bus, but a great deal has happened in between. Because of its careful integration, the bus ride has become a metaphor for knowledge and truth and for the superior importance of truth. Remembering the bus ride, listeners should be able to remember the rest. Such remembering would be one reward of an integrated whole.

An essential function of integration is control. Well-told stories quickly assume a life of their own. Total interpretive control is not possible. Narratives mean more, or are open to more interpretations, than any single preacher can either grasp or specify. It is also the case that narratives pass no meaning from teller to listener: "It is their nature to demand that we produce rather than consume them, and that we liberate them from local and provincial restrictions."[15] The narrative is something that happens between the narrator and the audience. The teller of the tale is not its only interpreter. Certain effects of this character of narrative have already been mentioned. It has been noted, for example, that personal stories sometimes seem to mean something other than what the narrator says they mean. In such cases, the listener has to listen to both tale and narrator and then make up his or her own mind. Another common effect of this character of narrative is that the listener's attention becomes fixated on the story or on particular elements in it. Integration of the story into the rest of the sermon can exert some necessary control. Integration can help keep listeners from remembering only the story.

Weatherhead again provides a helpful example. In his sermon "Let's Not Be Disgusted with Ourselves," Weatherhead talks about Christmas Day afternoon in his childhood home.[16] The focus is on Weatherhead's "beloved Scottish Presbyterian father," who would sit by the firelight after the Christmas dinner but who would let his heart be "at home in dear auld Scotland." Weatherhead's description of his father's homesickness is very moving and it would not be difficult for listeners to get lost in an old man's memories and tears. Nor would it seem difficult for listeners to simply forget about the sermon in order to think about childhood, or about parents now dead, or about Christmas days past. But Weatherhead keeps the listener's attention on the point of his story and he does so by integration. The sermon is based on Heb. 11:16, "They desire a better country, that is, an heavenly . . ." (KJV). The sermon contains not only the story of a childhood Christmas Day, but several other references as well. Weatherhead talks about Indian students attending City Temple who must long for the sights, sounds, food, and clothes of their native land. "I expect they dream of the day," he says, "when a ship lands them . . . so that . . . they can make a swift journey to their home, to where they really belong." He talks about a child at boarding school "lying awake the first night in a dormitory," and about the nights when many of us could not sleep and "under the bedclothes allowed ourselves just the ghost of a sob because we longed for home." He talks about the fast sale of books of poetry and books on nature, "symptoms of a desire for a better country that is heavenly." Weatherhead's story of his father is not lost among these other references, but it is buffered and controlled. By carefully integrating the Christmas Day story with the rest, he clearly indicates that the point is not his father but the longing for home of which his father's reverie is but one instance. Weatherhead refuses to let us dwell on his father or even on our own longing. Neither we nor our parents are the only ones away from home or sobbing under the bedclothes.

Integration of personal story with the rest of a sermon also lessens the chance of the story being heard as a piece of self-aggrandizement. Integrating can save the narrator from calling undue attention to himself or herself. An example of ego controlled by context is offered in Edmund Steimle's sermon "And How Does It All End?"[17] Steimle suggests that most people do not think about a resurrection from the dead "as if it were the most important news about your life and mine." He then admits that at least that is the way it is with him. He describes what happens when he pulls himself out of bed each morning and concludes, "Never once did I give even a passing thought to the resurrection from the dead." There is probably little chance that any reader would take this short self-reference as self-aggrandizement. Nonetheless, Steimle uses contextual safeguards. The self-reference is preceded by a general statement about all of us. It is followed immediately by a quote from Helmut Thielicke: "We don't *think* that way. . . . The bird of a cheerful breakfast in the hand is worth more than a couple of resurrections in the bush." Steimle's "I" is so closely sandwiched by "we" and "we" that neither the eye nor ear rests on what he says about himself.

This same pattern occurs in Steimle's sermon "Making Friends with Time."[18] Steimle claims that one of the ways in which we handle the problem of time and our bondage to it is by killing it. "You and I can be experts at that," he says. And then he tells how he killed time during a recent eight-hour automobile trip: "It was a lost day . . . nothing accomplished." Here again there is probably little chance that a listener would judge that Steimle is promoting himself. Here again, however, contextual safeguards are present. The first "I" is preceded by several sentences in which the subject is "we." And the brief "I" passage is followed by a longer paragraph describing common ways by which everyone kills time. Steimle is clearly present in the text but he is present as one of us. His "I" has been integrated with ours. He is no better and no worse than any listener. By such integration attention is drawn away from Steimle and put on humanity and the problem of time.

6
Occasions for
Self-Portrayal

No claim has been made in this book that personal story preaching is the only kind of preaching that is effective. To claim that would be an absurdity. There is too much evidence to the contrary. It has not even been claimed that the preacher's "I" must be present only in personal story form. There are several ways for the "I" to declare its presence in a sermon, and there is ample evidence that these other ways are effective vehicles for proclamation. I would not want to claim that the presence of the preacher's "I" in personal story is a necessity for each and every sermon. There may be occasions when personal story is irretrievable or when it seems unnecessary. There may also be occasions, however, when personal story seems to be the most appropriate form for the preacher's "I" to take.

THE NEED TO STATE CREDENTIALS

There are occasions when it seems important for preachers to state their credentials. Sometimes this is no more than a simple self-introduction. We preachers who are full-time teachers probably speak to groups of strangers more often than do parish pastors. Even so, most of us are involved in events where we are unknown to our audience except for a few sterile-sounding facts that appear in a bulletin or that are read from a sheet that we have sent ahead. On such occasions it seems important for us to disclose the person behind the stated facts. Preaching is a personal transaction, and one thing that we can do to encourage the transaction is to make ourselves more fully available by means of personal story. Not any story, of course, but a story that meets the requirements of *simplicitas* and *scopus*. On certain occasions of this sort it may also be important for preachers to announce how they feel about standing in front of strangers for the task at hand. "Here I am, the stranger in your midst," says Frederick Buechner to a graduating class.[1] "I wouldn't have the brass to stand here before you now if the only words I had to speak were the ones I had cooked up for the occasion."[2] "I wrote and tried to withdraw," Jürgen Moltmann tells a combined conference of the handicapped and nonhandicapped.[3] "I am not the proper person for it: I myself am not handicapped. . . . Let the people who are handicapped do the talking themselves!"[4] Neither Buechner nor Moltmann chose to announce their perspective by personal story, but they might have. At the very least, they affirm our potential need for stating credentials by the introduction of ourselves beyond newspaper announcement or biographical rehearsal.

A simple introduction can also be used to state the preacher's lack of credentials for the event at hand. Moltmann does this when he tells how he feels as a nonhandicapped person addressing "The Liberation and Acceptance of the Handicapped."[5] This was not the only occasion on which Moltmann expressed such an awareness of his limitations. Responding to an invitation to speak on "The Ministry of the Whole Church to the World," for example, Moltmann readily admits: "I am talking as someone living in the industrial West; as a member of what is known as bourgeois society; as a male . . . , as a professor of theology . . . , and finally as a Christian living in Germany, a member of a Protestant established church."[6] Obviously, such an admission of limitation does not eliminate the limitation nor does it excuse Moltmann from being self-critical throughout his sermon or lecture. It does, however, establish Moltmann as a person who is aware not only of the subject matter, but also of himself and his audience in relation to the subject matter. It further establishes him as a person of unusual openness. In detailing his lack of credentials in such a self-critical and open way, Moltmann actually secures them.

Certainly Moltmann is not the only preacher who shares his limitation of experience and perspective in such an open way. He is like countless others, however, who share by personal assertion rather than by personal story. While the listener or reader assumes that an awareness of limitations makes some difference in the way a speaker now views the subject, the difference is not clear. I want to suggest that story brings subject and limitation together in a way that clarifies the difference that self-awareness makes. I am thinking, for example, of a sermon that I heard in my classroom recently. It was given by a man on the Advent text that tells the story of the pregnant Mary's visit to Elizabeth (Luke 1:39–45). The male student began by telling the story of his wife's pregnancy. He showed us a verbal picture of him and his wife at the doctor's office when they were told the good news. We saw them fixing a nursery corner in their student apartment, buying a hundred items that expectant parents need to get, dreaming together about the future. They did so much and experienced so much together. But there were some things, of course, that only his wife could do and experience firsthand. It was her body that was examined at the doctor's office. It was her body that changed to nurture the new life within. It was her body that moved slowly toward the moment of delivery. "When it comes to expectant waiting," the student said, "my wife knows something that I do not." The story introduced us to the student's awareness of his own maleness. Pregnancy and giving birth are two things about which males have no firsthand experience. The story also told us that this sermon on Advent waiting would be different because of the student's recognized limits. My memory tells me that most sermons preached by men in Advent focus on preparation. This sermon, informed by the preacher's boundaries, would focus on waiting in the expectation of new life.

There are times when preachers need to state their credentials beyond what I have called a simple introduction. This need is not met by an announcement of "how I got to be here." It is met rather by an announcement of "the right by which I say these things to you." P. T. Forsyth responds to this need when he "ventures" to speak of himself when "addressing young men who have the ministry before them."[7] This piece of personal narrative adds weight to Forsyth's conclusions. The narrative does this by demonstrating that Forsyth's conclusions are the result of "thirty years given to progressive thought in connection . . . with a pulpit and the care of souls."[8] In other words, Forsyth has earned the right to say what he does. In much the same way, Colin Morris refers to his attempts "to speak prophetically within a situation of racial and political conflict."[9] He is preaching to pastors about the tensions of ministry and how they can be torn apart trying to do justice to both the priestly and prophetic roles. "I can speak with authority," he says. "I have had to live with the consequent damage done to the church and see the eroding away of my priestly authority."[10]

Preachers need to demonstrate that they share a life common to their audiences. They do share a common life, and when they "preach from out of the memory of what they have experienced . . . they will make the discovery that they are speaking to men's condition and their preaching is received."[11] So it is important for Karl Barth preaching at Basel Prison to demonstrate to the inmates that he is not "a half-saint" who has never done a wrong "that brought him before the judge."[12] Barth wants the inmates to know that he understands wrongdoing, and judges, and penalties as much as they do. A convinced Christian, Barth insists, knows that he or she must appear before the most severe judge there is and must expiate for what one has been, thought, said, and done. Therefore, Barth urges, "Don't think and say of me: 'Well, what idle talk!' "[13] Barth's brief narrative of the "convinced Christian" does not assume the form of a personal story. Strictly speaking, it is not even a narrative, but it illustrates the need preachers have to supply the credentials of a common life. I chose it also because it represents the halfway point between assertion and personal story. It does not fully represent what is being encouraged in this book, but it goes far beyond other attempts at establishing common ground. "I know the things that happen," Paul Scherer insists, "the loss and the loneliness and the pain."[14] But all he offers is the assertion, unsupported by a single instance. The reader of his sermon, if not the listener in his congregation, is left wondering whether he knows "the things that happen" or not.

I also chose the example from Barth because I think it illustrates one of the ways a preacher can reach across sociocultural barriers. Barth is not a prisoner in the same way the members of his audience are. We do not know whether or not he has ever stood before a judge in a court of law or ever had a penalty assessed against him. Certainly the story of a parking violation and fine, if there were one, would not work on this occasion. Even if Barth had been a prisoner of war and could talk out of that experience, the commonality between him and the inmates would still not be established. They are in prison now and he is not. He needs to find a dimension in which he stands as convicted as they, in which he is as unable to walk free as they are. This he finds at the level of Christian narrative, the story of the convinced Christian under the judgment of God.

Much more in line with the kind of personal story encouraged by this book is a sermon by Frederick Buechner.[15] The sermon is based in part on Deut. 6:4–7, the command given to wilderness-wandering Israel to "love the Lord your God with all your heart, and with all your soul, and with all your might (KJV)." By what right, one can imagine Buechner asking, can I speak to a wilderness people about the command to love God in the wilderness? The only possible answer is, "Because there isn't one of us who hasn't wandered there, lost, and who will not wander there again before our time is done."[16] Buechner rightly determines that the commonality of that wandering must be demonstrated. And so he tells of a time when his wilderness was "a strange city three thousand miles from home." Buechner reveals the contours of this wilderness in a few deft strokes: a hospital, a loved one as terrified of death as of life, visits day after day, the danger of death. We believe him when he says he "passed beyond grief, beyond terror, all but beyond hope."

Preachers need to demonstrate that they share a common human life. Yet some might suggest that it cannot be done. Your story is not mine, nor is my story yours. Barth does not share a life common to the inmates at Basel Prison. And not all who hear or read about Buechner's wilderness have stood in a hospital room in a strange city three thousand miles from home. Nonetheless, we want to claim that Barth, the inmates at Basel, you, and I share a common life. Our lives are not common at the level of surface details. But they are common, as has been said before, at the level of fundamental experience and existential feelings. We all know what it is to be accused, judged, and found guilty. And we all have experienced strangeness, helplessness, and loss. These are primordial human experiences. As Willa Cather has said, "There are only two or three human stories, and they go on repeating themselves as fiercely as if they had never happened before."[17]

A preacher's personal story must describe fundamental (primordial) experience if it is to demonstrate that a common life is shared by preacher and congregation. In this way the preacher offers his or her credentials, his or her right to speak. But this is not the only right that the preacher needs to claim. The preacher must also testify to the good news of Christ and the way in which this good news illumines and transforms the shared life. This right can also be demonstrated by personal story. The preacher can show that he or she knows the light as well as the darkness and can give a firsthand report of the fact that the light banishes the darkness. Moltmann's sermon "The Liberation and Acceptance of the Handicapped" offers a good example of what I mean. Moltmann makes the claim that "self-love evokes strength of soul, and strength of soul gives us power to move mountains."[18] But how, he asks, does a person come to love, and not to despise, himself or herself? In terms of what we have been saying, he has set quite an agenda for himself. He needs to demonstrate his right to speak to those who despise themselves. And he needs to demonstrate that he has the right to point the way to a strength-evoking self-love. He does both by sharing the story of his experiences "in the misery of a dirty hut in a prisoner-of-war camp in 1945."[19] He was overcome by a deadly depression. "I became ill. I didn't get up any more. I didn't want to go on living." He had lost all earlier hopes. But then, what he calls "a miracle" happened. Friends came to his aid. He discovered that there was someone who loved him, believed in him, waited for him. As soon as he sensed this, he crept out of his corner and began to love himself again. Moltmann's experience gives him the right to tell his audience: "Because God loves us, we should love ourselves." It is clear that Moltmann does not expect his sermon/lecture to work a miracle for his audience, for those caught in the despair of self-hate. He honestly admits how easy his conclusion sounds and how difficult it is to put into practice. But he has demonstrated his right to say it and it holds out promise and possibility for those who fear: If it happened to him in his difficulties, it could also happen to me.

THE NEED TO WITNESS

For some time now preachers have had difficulty in distinguishing the kerygmatic and didactic roles of preaching. The difficulty lies more with the nature of their audiences than it does with any theoretical disability. The normal audience for most preachers is that of the parishes they serve. Theory declares that the aim of their preaching, therefore, should be edification. Most Sunday listeners are baptized members of the Body of Christ. What they are in need of is renewal and growth in the gospel. But "renewal" in the sense of "refreshment" or "rejuvenation" does not adequately describe the condition of most

Christian communities today. Definitions of "renewal" that point toward "beginning again" seem more accurate.

Perhaps this observation does not need to be elaborated upon, yet it seems important to do so. For the last forty years, some say, the church has been undergoing a process of dechristianization. There is, as Domenico Grasso asserted, "a kind of paganism within its own borders."[20] Not only do many Christians live at war with the principles they profess, but they live a life and vision which is not Christian at all. The values by which many Christians actually live have been regularly identified with Christ, but they are not the values of the gospel. Concerns of family, career, standard of living, and health rule more Christian lives than do concerns of renunciation, self-giving, and reconciliation. As it is reported in *Habits of the Heart*, "Relatively few middle-class urbanites described themselves to us as 'children of God,' created in his image and likeness, bound by his commandments, and inspired by his love."[21] In a more inclusive sweep, Carl Braaten has said, "The trouble with Christianity in the West . . . is not that there are too few church members; it is rather that there are teeming millions of them who have succeeded in so redefining what is Christian, that the Church's faith is cut down to the size of the world's idealism."[22]

My point is not to argue the accuracy of such harsh observations. It is only to indicate that the goal of even parish preaching may not be simply the nurturing of committed lives. Not many would disagree with Helmut Thielicke's assessment of "our contemporaries" as those who have come to "distrust *all* forms of public speech, *every* kind of 'speaking on someone else's orders'—and hence what the *church* says too."[23] And, we might add, these "contemporaries" are within the church as well as without. These comments are not meant as criticism of the church, but only as facing the facts. Today's congregation may not be hostile. But it is a congregation that is skeptical and, to some degree, unhearing.

I want to suggest that such a situation pushes the witnessing dimension of preaching to the foreground. Thielicke himself acknowledges that it is only when the speaker as witness comes forward that people will regard the speaker as credible and worth listening to.[24] I also want to suggest that one of the most effective forms for such witnessing is that of personal story. Personal story declares that what is confessed is personally owned by the speaker.[25] It also invites the listener to identify rather than argue. Identification and empathy are more likely to overcome resistance than argument. With personal story, the speaker at least stands a chance of making his or her position humanly comprehensible to the listener.[26]

It is not surprising that the introduction to a relatively recent book of "sermons for evangelical outreach" speaks of "sharing the biography of Jesus Christ in the context of our own biographies."[27] Nor is it surprising that many of the fifteen sermons in this volume contain personal story. One sermon begins, "It happened a few weeks ago on the final leg of a flying trip at the end of a long week."[28] Another begins: "I would venture to say that I am the only Lutheran pastor here who started out as a Jew and thought about becoming a Roman Catholic priest. . . . Let me elaborate."[29] And still another begins: "Two members of the congregation had been after me to go fishing with them. . . . I finally agreed to go."[30] These preachers would probably agree with Alfred Krass: "Storytelling is a mode of communication that yields nothing to preaching in its faithfulness to Scripture, but avoids the Bible-pounding dogmatism that characterizes many evangelistic sermons."[31]

In *The Significance of Silence*, Leslie Weatherhead has two sermons on going to church. The audience for both seems to be that specified in "Why People Don't Go to Church." It is made up of those of "you who have drifted away from God, given up all attempt to pray perhaps, kept away from his house, shut yourself off from his love, and left him out of your life."[32] In "Why People Do Go to Church," Weatherhead tells of two young women of his acquaintance. One's dream of becoming a surgeon was shattered by a bomb explosion which, even after thirty-five operations, left her with only the glimmer of sight in one eye. The other is confined to a mental hospital for the rest of her life. Though there are periods when she is "entirely sane and pleads to be taken home," she cannot be left alone. "Twice she has tried to take her own life, and there always exists the danger of her attacking others."[33] Both young women suffer a need so deep that "no human resourcefulness is an adequate reply." But why, Weatherhead asks, do people who have lost everything still go to church? They do, he says, because God is the only comfort for them. Not a God who offers explanations, but a God who is himself crucified, a God "who brings his children through their dread sufferings with finally nothing lost."[34] Weatherhead does not try to outdo God in this sermon. That is to say, he does not try to explain human suffering, nor does he attempt to argue people back to church. He simply tells his story of the two young women and allows that story to bear witness. He knows the appropriateness of personal story for the audience he needs to touch.

THE NEED TO BE PROPHETIC

In his Lyman Beecher lectures on preaching, James Claypool refers to the prophetic as "one of the most delicate challenges of the ministry."[35] He asks how it is possible to deal with a sick situation in ways that will heal rather than make matters worse. He discovered in the practice of ministry that the strategy of pronouncement and condemnation did not work. The situations he wanted to change only became more rigid and resistant to change. Honestly admitting that he personally was both attracted to and repulsed by the prospect of change, he learned the lesson of Matt. 7:5, "First take the log out of your own eye, and then you will see clearly to take the speck out of your brother's eye." Attracted by this alternative to pronouncement and condemnation, Claypool began to "grapple openly with the darkness that is in my own life." He discovered the power of such personal story to lift a sense of shame from others and to inject hope into the situation.

Others have discovered the same power of personal story. Richard Jensen, for example, recommends the autobiographical format when dealing with highly charged social, political, and ethical issues.[36] He does this because autobiography has the potential for creating distance. Listeners are safe. Space is given for them to move with the speaker without being forced to do so. It invites them to identify with the process by which the speaker has arrived at a conclusion, and it allows them the chance to make up their own minds.

As Ronald J. Allen prepares for a sermon on the parable of the Good Samaritan (Luke 10:25–37), he writes, "My situation is hardly parallel to that of the Samaritan."[37] Allen is a white, male, middle-class Christian. In spite of that, he knows what it feels like to have his ideas "completely (and rudely) put down," to have someone angry with him, "to have children question him about the skin graft on his forehead." He is dealing with the parable at the level of existential feelings and will preach to the same level in his listeners. He wants his listeners to identify the Samaritan in themselves, to identify their own wound-edness. But Allen also wants his listeners to be able to experience the kind of resources with which they can go and do as the Samaritan did. He needs to show them a picture of one who, like the Samaritan, remembered what it was like to be wounded and thus showed com-passion. And so he tells them the story of his week at Koinonia Farm, and of Miss Gussie, whose weathered clapboard house he helped paint. It was Allen's first time as the only white among a large number of blacks. "My stomach was knotted. My palm was sweaty. My leg quiv-ered ever so slightly." But Miss Gussie "remembered what it was like to be lying by the side of the road." And it was Miss Gussie who came forward and eased the tension by putting her arms around Allen and the others.

The story of Miss Gussie creates the distance that Jensen applauds. I do not have to go to Americus, Georgia, and put myself into a tension-filled situation. I do not have to accept Allen's claim that woundedness becomes a source of healing power. All that is asked of me is that I listen to the story. The story reminds me of my own woundedness and of the compassion shown me. It also suggests a real possibility for my future behavior. It does this without putting me on the defensive and without making me feel like arguing. I could always argue against the principle of woundedness/compassion, but I cannot argue away Allen's experience and the compassionate behavior of Miss Gussie. I am moved by Allen's portrayal of himself and I am moved by Miss Gussie's sen-sitivity and her response to what she feels in Allen's nervous dis-ease.

The volume *Preaching in the Witnessing Community* contains several sermons identified by the editor as sermons that "offer guidance to the people of God as they seek ways to make faith concretely active in the spheres of the world's life."[38] One of these is a sermon by Charles Rice entitled "An Uncommonly Common Grace."[39] The sermon is based on John 4:1–26, the story of Jesus' meeting at the well with the woman of Samaria. Nothing is said about the exact situation for which it was prepared or where it may have been preached. But Rice specifies his audience. They are people who would most likely avoid this woman who was "outcast even by outcasts." They are people that Rice wants to encourage to "keep cool and, at the same time, care" in the midst of those from "across the tracks." And so he tells the story of his visit to the North Carolina farm of a friend's parents. It is a story about what happened when three other guests arrived for a five o'clock dinner. One of these guests was dressed like a Gypsy, and another like an American Indian. The third guest, a "thirtyish man" wore "tie-dyed rainbow jeans, orange shirt, and hair to match." Rice was fearful about the reaction of his farm friends to such a bizarre group. But there was only an almost-invisible initial shock and a few long glances by an amused Grandma. The three were fed and were "made to be at home." By the hosts' graciousness, Rice concludes, the meal itself was an act of real human communion. "Daily bread can at any time become the bread of life, just as water in the well could tell of God's great gift revealed in Jesus, lover of Samaritans, hippies, and the likes of us."[40]

As far as we know, neither of these sermons was preached on the occasion of some specific social or congregational crisis. Yet they are examples of prophetic preaching. They deal with the sickness of bigotry and provinciality in ways that heal rather than make matters worse. In both cases the preachers speak as persons who know the darkness in their own lives. Their personal stories create a safety zone where we can listen without being run over and where we do not have to be on constant guard against attack. We are forced to no conclusion, although we are clearly pointed toward one. We are neither pronounced against nor condemned. We are not told what to do, but we are shown possibilities for action.

7
Checklist for Using Self-Portrayal

The effective use of personal story in preaching demands awareness, skill, and practice. On the one hand, personal stories must avoid narcissism, privatism, and isolation. On the other hand, personal stories must proclaim Christ, place their hearers under the judgment and grace of God, be integral parts of the sermons in which they appear, and accurately express the biblical text. I have made suggestions throughout this book as to how an effective use of personal story can be accomplished. These suggestions can serve as a kind of guideline inventory. I summarize them here and offer them as a checklist for developing the awareness, skill, and practice that are so crucial.

1. Personal stories are of various types. It is important to know which type you intend and why. Each type varies in its special features, function, and degree of self-disclosure.

Some questions to ask:
   a. What type of personal story will you share?
   —illustration
   —reminiscence
   —confession
   —self-portrayal
   b. Is the type of personal story you intend adequate for your purposes? See the table on p. 76.
   c. If your intended story is not one of self-portrayal, could it be developed into one?

2. Stories of self-portrayal are distinguished by three essential components. Without the presence of all three the story will fall short of its potential.

To ensure that your story is one of self-portrayal, the following questions must be answered affirmatively:

    a. Does the story convey your sense of discovery about yourself, the world, and God?

    b. Does the story focus on the self as thinking, feeling, and willing?

    c. Does the story reveal you as you are related to the lives of others and to God?

3. Personal stories in the pulpit must be used as vehicles of Christian proclamation. Stories are safeguarded as proclamation when they remain subject to both the "news about Christ" and the biblical text.

Some indications of failure as proclamation:

    a. Is your story so general that it basically ignores the text?

    b. Does your story trivialize the text by failing to offer a sense of personal discovery or by failing to coincide with the text and the purpose of the sermon?

    c. Does your story only parallel the text? Are they connected only by a similarity of words or experience?

Some indications of success as proclamation:

    a. Is your story a contemporary equivalent of the text?

    b. Does your story clarify the biblical message and make it accessible?

    c. Does your story raise significant questions about the text that readies a congregation to hear it in a new way?

    d. Does your story offer access to answers within the text to questions raised by the text itself?

    e. Does your story allow listeners to enter the text and to see both it and themselves from the inside?

4. Personal stories must be integral parts of the sermons in which they appear. Such stories should inform the rest of the sermon, even as they are informed by the sermon's developing themes.

To ensure integration, the following questions should be answered in the affirmative:

    a. Is the story necessary for the sermon?

    b. Does the sermon correctly interpret the story?

    c. Is the story carried through? Is it referred to again? Is its language used? Is it reflected upon?

    d. Do story and developing theme tell the same story?

5. There are some occasions when personal story seems to be the most effective form for proclamation to assume. There are times when the preacher needs to state his or her credentials, when there is special need to bear witness, or when a prophetic word is to be preached.

   a. If the occasion demands credentials, how will your story state yours?

     —self-introduction

     —sharing your limit of experience and perspective

     —indicating the life you share in common

     —clarifying your right to speak on the subject at hand

     —reaching across sociocultural barriers

     —personally testifying to the good news of Christ

   b. If the occasion calls for personal witness, does your story declare that you personally own what is confessed?

   c. If the occasion necessitates a prophetic word, will your personal story do the following?

     —clarify the process by which you arrived at your conclusion

     —allow listeners the chance to make up their own minds

     —show that you know the darkness in your own life

TABLE 1
TYPES OF FIRST-PERSON STORIES

	Special features	Functions	Degree of self-disclosure
ILLUSTRATION	1. Little detail 2. Focus on general "truth" 3. Recount private events	To clarify	Little or none
REMINISCENCE	1. More detail 2. Focus on memory 3. Recount private events	To appeal	Self as thinking (remembering)
CONFESSION	1. Little detail 2. Focus on self and God 3. Recount private events	To give an example	Self as feeling
SELF-PORTRAYAL	1. Most detail 2. Focus on self and God/world 3. Recount private/ public events	To clarify, appeal, serve as exemplar (or as model), attain companionship	Self as thinking, feeling, willing

Appendix 1
Edmund A. Steimle

This excerpt is from Edmund A. Steimle, *God the Stranger: Reflections About Resurrection* (Philadelphia: Fortress Press, 1979), page 15. It is discussed on pages 25–26.

Or contrariwise, the stranger may be recognizable when you and I respond in love and concern and thoughtfulness to the needs of another. As John says in the Fourth Gospel, "He that wills to *do* shall know." I can remember in my last parish that when I was down in the dumps, discouraged, uncertain of the reality of God, I would go to the hospital and visit with patients from my parish, offering what I could of reassurance and comfort and hope in God's presence and care, and then the God who may have been a stranger to me earlier became recognizable in the breaking of bread.

But it may be that he becomes recognizable on the lips of unlikely people. It was many years ago, shortly after the end of World War II, and I was in the shop of a friendly neighborhood tailor whose name was Mr. Birnbaum. And he stopped me as I was leaving and said in his thick accent, "Mr. Steimle, I have a problem. As you know, I am a Jew and my wife, she is a Christian. Her brother was a violent Nazi when we were in Germany. He hated me and did nothing to help us. He was happy to get rid of us when we came over here. But now he is in a prison camp and he has written us asking us to send him some food. My wife, she says No, we send him nothing. But I say Yes, we should send him something. What do you think, Mr. Steimle?" I don't know how you would have felt, but I felt humble and ashamed. Ashamed of his Christian wife possibly, but even more ashamed of myself for being unprepared to find the stranger God recognizable on the lips of a pleasant Jewish neighborhood tailor.

Appendix 2
Martin Luther King, Jr.

This excerpt is taken from Martin Luther King, Jr., *Strength to Love* (Philadelphia: Fortress Press, 1981), 112–14. It is discussed on pages 26–28.

At times we may feel that we do not need God, but on the day when the storms of disappointment rage, the winds of disaster blow, and the tidal waves of grief beat against our lives, if we do not have a deep and patient faith our emotional lives will be ripped to shreds. There is so much frustration in the world because we have relied on gods rather than God. We have genuflected before the god of science only to find that it has given us the atomic bomb, producing fears and anxieties that science can never mitigate. We have worshipped the god of pleasure only to discover that thrills play out and sensations are short-lived. We have bowed before the god of money only to learn that there are such things as love and friendship that money cannot buy and that in a world of possible depressions, stock market crashes, and bad business investments, money is a rather uncertain deity. These transitory gods are not able to save us or bring happiness to the human heart.

Only God is able. It is faith in him that we must rediscover. With this faith we can transform bleak and desolate valleys into sunlit paths of joy and bring new light into the dark caverns of pessimism. Is someone here moving toward the twilight of life and fearful of that which we call death? Why be afraid? God is able. Is someone here on the brink of despair because of the death of a loved one, the breaking of a marriage, or the waywardness of a child? Why despair? God is able to give you the power to endure that which cannot be changed. Is someone here anxious because of bad health? Why be anxious? Come what may, God is able.

As I come to the conclusion of my message, I would wish you to permit a personal experience. The first twenty-four years of my life were years packed with fulfilment. I had no basic problems or burdens. Because of concerned and loving parents who provided for my every need, I sallied through high school, college, theological school, and graduate school without interruption. It was not until I became a part of the leadership of the Montgomery bus protest that I was actually confronted with the trials of life. Almost immediately after the protest had been undertaken, we began to receive threatening telephone calls and letters in our home. Sporadic in the beginning, they increased day after day. At first I took them in my stride, feeling that they were the work of a few hotheads who would become discouraged after they discovered that we would not fight back. But as the weeks passed, I realized that many of the threats were in earnest. I felt myself faltering and growing in fear.

After a particularly strenuous day, I settled in bed at a late hour. My wife had already fallen asleep and I was about to doze off when the telephone rang. An angry voice said, "Listen, nigger, we've taken all we want from you. Before next week you'll be sorry you ever came to Montgomery." I hung up, but I could not sleep. It seemed that all of my fears had come down on me at once. I had reached the saturation point.

I got out of bed and began to walk the floor. Finally, I went to the kitchen and heated a pot of coffee. I was ready to give up. I tried to think of a way to move out of the picture without appearing to be a coward. In this state of exhaustion, when my courage had almost gone, I determined to take my problem to God. My head in my hands, I bowed over the kitchen table and prayed aloud. The words I spoke to God that midnight are still vivid in my memory. "I am here taking a stand for what I believe is right. But now I am afraid. The people are looking to me for leadership, and if I stand before them without strength and courage, they too will falter. I am at the end of my powers. I have nothing left. I've come to the point where I can't face it alone."

At that moment I experienced the presence of the Divine as I had never before experienced him. It seemed as though I could hear the quiet assurance of an inner voice, saying, "Stand up for righteousness, stand up for truth. God will be at your side forever." Almost at once my fears began to pass from me. My uncertainty disappeared. I was ready to face anything. The outer situation remained the same, but God had given me inner calm.

Three nights later, our home was bombed. Strangely enough, I accepted the word of the bombing calmly. My experience with God had given me a new strength and trust. I knew now that God is able to give us the interior resources to face the storms and problems of life.

Let this affirmation be our ringing cry. It will give us courage to face the uncertainties of the future. It will give our tired feet new strength as we continue our forward stride toward the city of freedom. When our days become dreary with low-hovering clouds and our nights become darker than a thousand midnights, let us remember that there is a great benign Power in the universe whose name is God, and he is able to make a way out of no way, and transform dark yesterdays into bright tomorrows. This is our hope for becoming better men. This is our mandate for seeking to make a better world.

Appendix 3
John Vannorsdall

This excerpt is taken from John Vannorsdall, "The Bus," in *Preaching on Peace*, ed. Ronald J. Sider and Darrel J. Brubaker (Philadelphia: Fortress Press, 1982), 65–69. It is discussed on pages 57–58.

> I am the good shepherd. The good shepherd lays down his life for the sheep. He who is a hireling and not a shepherd, whose own the sheep are not, sees the wolf coming and leaves the sheep and flees; and the wolf snatches them and scatters them. He flees because he is a hireling and cares nothing for the sheep. I am the good shepherd; I know my own and my own know me, as the Father knows me and I know the Father; and I lay down my life for the sheep. And I have other sheep, that are not of this fold; I must bring them also, and they will heed my voice. So there shall be one flock, one shepherd.
>
> John 10:11–16

When I came out of the train station, I could see a bus approaching, so I joined the crowd at the bus stop for a ride to the Green. The driver opened the door and said something, but only the people at the head of the line could hear what she said. By the time I was close enough to drop my coins into the fare box, the problem had become known to everyone: two young boys who needed transfers had already dropped their money through the slot before they discovered that the driver had no transfers. I gathered from the conversation that the driver had no way of getting their money out of the box again, and that one of the two boys had no money left for boarding the next bus that would take him to his destination.

It was at this point that some of the passengers got involved. One observed to the driver: "There's a bus pulling up behind us"—which prompted the driver's suggestion: "You fellows get on the bus behind me and just tell them you've already paid."

"That driver ain't gonna believe those boys," objected another passenger. There was a murmur of agreement.

Our driver looked around at us helplessly as though to say, "Now you folks know I'm not supposed to leave this bus." But there was something in the face of the heavyset lady across from me, and of the man with the lunch pail, which seemed to convey: "It's all right, lady; we'll take care of the bus."

So our driver got off, walked quickly to the trailing bus, got some transfers, and returned and gave them to the two boys—who seemed relieved. Off we went with the usual roar while the lady sitting next to me shouted across the aisle, "She's new, but she's gonna do all right."

Two things are important about this episode. The first is that the passengers about me that day were very knowledgeable about buses. They knew the importance of a transfer, that the driver was unable to get money out of the box, and that she was reluctant to leave her bus. They knew, too, that the driver behind wouldn't believe the boys, and that our driver was new. In fact, I was the least knowledgeable passenger on board—a full two blocks beyond my stop before someone showed me how to push the signal button for getting off.

Now, it's all right that I'm not knowledgeable about buses—because I know some other things, and so do you. We are all knowledgeable about some things. Yale is a great knowledge factory. *Veritas*—truth— is our motto, but knowledge is our game. The two are not the same.

Knowledge is how to get a bus to stop; it's learning to describe the forces that powered the Westward movement in the United States; it's the capacity to observe, analyze, generalize, and test. To be knowledgeable is to have mastered a variety of processes, fingering, and irregular verbs. Knowledge is the capacity to recognize sounds and patterns, to distinguish ends from means, to remember what *has been*—for the purpose of either repeating or avoiding it, or to predict on the basis of what has been what *might be*.

Knowledge is ubiquitous. It facilitates a bus ride, and it fills the seas and the air of the South Atlantic with ships and planes. But a jump jet is knowledge, not truth.

Only fools spurn knowledge. Religious people cherish it. It is important to us that God *knows* us. The promise of today's text makes a difference: "I am the good shepherd; I know my own, and my own know me." "O God, thou knowest my folly; the wrongs I have done are not hidden from thee," wrote the psalmist. "O Lord, thou hast searched me and known me! Thou knowest when I sit down and when I rise up; thou discernest my thoughts from afar. . . . If I take the wings of the morning and dwell in the uttermost parts of the sea, even there thy hand shall lead me, and thy right hand shall hold me."

These words have been rehearsed in so many prisons, in distant airports, in trains and buses—by people who stand alone at the rails of ships, who walk the night streets, who lie in their beds when the hospital grows quiet, when the house is silent, when everyone has gone. "I am the good shepherd; I know my own, and my own know me." "Yea, though I walk through the valley of the shadow. . . ." "For now," wrote Paul, "we see through a glass darkly, but then face to face. Now I know in part; then I shall understand fully, even as I have been fully understood."

Important in these passages is the affirmation that God knows us. The witness is not about how much or how little we know of God— that comes more fully later. Faith *begins* with the affirmation that we are known and that there is nothing hidden: the worst is out—and still we have a Shepherd! To live convinced that God knows us is no small thing.

But there is something more important than knowledge, whether it be the knowledge of buses, or warships and planes, or even of God's knowledge of us. The second thing I learned on the bus that day was that the people there *cared* about what happened. The man with the lunch pail didn't want the boys to be stuck far from home. The heavyset lady didn't want them to face an unbelieving driver in the bus behind. And the lady next to me cared whether our driver, who was new at her job, would make it. Their knowledge of buses was not *the* truth, but their knowledge was placed in the service of truth, and truth was in their caring.

In the South Atlantic [Falkland Islands war, 1982], where knowledge is everywhere visible, truth is not. Truth is so absent in the South Atlantic that half the world doesn't know whether to laugh or to weep at the absurdity of it. Weep mostly, I think—in part for those who are dying, but in part for ourselves at the realization that human beings can be so knowledgeable and still engage in such stupidity. The people on the bus would do better. They would understand about pride, and the importance of preserving it for both countries, and they would find a way to keep both flags flying. They would do that because they cared enough about what happened to young soldiers and sailors, to the Islanders, and even to the sheep. And their caring, whatever the outcome, would be the lasting truth that would survive the current debacle in the South Atlantic.

Caring is the central affirmation concerning the Good Shepherd. Not just that he knows the sheep, which is important, but that he lays down his life for the sheep, which is crucial. This is no hireling, no shepherd-for-wages. When the cost of shepherding is greater than the wages, the hireling flees and leaves the sheep to the wolves. The Good Shepherd, not being a hireling, gives what wages can never buy.

But there's more to it than that. This Shepherd is neither British nor Argentinian, neither white nor black, neither first world nor third world. He always has sheep that are "not of this fold"—and the longing intention that these other sheep too be equally, and rightly, cared for.

Truth, wrote Joseph Sittler, frees us from the illusion that knowledge is redemptive. Knowledge makes the buses run; it informs us about how to get on and off. But truth makes human beings human. It reaches out to two small boys. Truth suggests transfers from the trailer. Truth assures the driver that no one will steal the bus. Truth does not demean a driver for being new, but wishes her well.

Veritas is our motto, but knowledge is our business, and it would be foolish to deny the importance of knowledge. But once more we engage in the organized slaughter of human beings, a carnage enhanced by the use of the latest devices of science, the best our knowledge can provide. In doing so, we demonstrate that we are little possessed of truth, that capacity for caring about one another which is our greatest joy, that which makes us most fully human. We have made a choice: believing that we are incapable of caring for and about one another, we have chosen to defend ourselves with the most deadly devices knowledge can provide—which, in time of crisis, means that we go to war. Why do we do this? Why do we believe that we are incapable of caring about one another? Why—when even the people on a bus, also strangers to one another, find it entirely possible to enjoy and practice truth!

Christians, some of us at least, are accused of being naive about human nature and about the so-called inevitability of war. But the issue is precisely at that point—the matter of inevitability. Christians are called precisely in order to see things differently—that is the meaning of repentance. We worship the God who in Christ made the blind see and the deaf hear, who dispossessed demons and taught us to believe that change is possible. We are even enabled to believe that peace is possible, that there are true shepherds and not only hirelings, that a man with a lunch pail is willing to look after the bus.

As Martin Luther might well have said: it is the devil's own device that when the world, like Humpty Dumpty, falls off the wall, each of us runs for cover, locks and bolts the door of our heart, and begins the long involution toward the imprisonment of the self. Knowledgeable about survival, we buy up what we need for the furnishing of our cave, let fall an iron curtain over the window of our souls, and, armed with the defenses of our class, keep watch against those who would invade our prison.

And the truth is not in us.

Truth is a Shepherd who walks in no man's land unafraid and gently rattles the iron curtain at the window of our souls to see if perhaps we won't come out—to walk with him among Humpty Dumpty's pieces and begin to do with compassion and care what all the King's Harriers and all the Junta's soldiers will not be able to do.

He is the truth which frees us from the illusion that knowledge is redemptive.

Truth is in buses.

Notes

2. TYPES OF PERSONAL STORY

1. Karl Barth, *Deliverance to thc Captives*, trans. Marguerite Wieser (New York: Harper & Brothers, 1961), 60–66.

2. Ibid., 64.

3. See, e.g., Charles Smyth, *The Art of Preaching: A Practical Survey of Preaching in the Church of England 747–1939* (London: SPCK, 1953), 108–9.

4. Hugh Latimer, *Sermons by Hugh Latimer*, ed. George Elwes Corrie (Cambridge: University Press, 1844), 101.

5. James S. Stewart, *The Winds of the Spirit* (Nashville: Abingdon Press, 1968), 123.

6. Barth, *Deliverance to the Captives*, 37.

7. See, e.g., Paul Delany, *British Autobiography in the Seventeenth Century* (Boston and London: Routledge & Kegan Paul, 1969), 32–37.

8. Georges Gusdorf, "Conditions and Limits of Autobiography," in *Autobiography: Essays Theoretical and Critical*, ed. James Olney (Princeton: Princeton University Press, 1980), 44.

9. William J. O'Brien, "Toward Understanding Original Sin in Augustine's 'Confessions,' " *Thought* (December 1974): 437.

10. See Francis Hart, "Notes for an Anatomy of Modern Autobiography," *New Literary History* 1 (Spring 1970): 491.

11. In this regard it is interesting to note Jürgen Moltmann's stated intention for his autobiographical essay: "This story of conflict can certainly provide other people with reasons for beginning to become a Christian . . ." *Experiences of God*, trans. Margaret Kohl (Philadelphia: Fortress Press, 1980), 4.

12. Leslie D. Weatherhead, *The Significance of Silence and Other Sermons* (Nashville: Abingdon-Cokesbury Press, 1945), 103–12.

13. Ibid., 117.

14. Roy Pascal, *Design and Truth in Autobiography* (Cambridge: Harvard University Press, 1960), 98.

15. "Lillian Hellman and the Strategy of the 'Other,' " in *Women's Autobiography: Essays in Criticism*, ed. Estelle Jelinek (Bloomington: Indiana University Press, 1980), 163.

16. Quoted in Wayne C. Booth, *The Rhetoric of Fiction* (Chicago: University of Chicago Press, 1970), 237. Richard Wright may speak for many listeners: "One feels not so much alone when, from a distant witness, supporting evidence comes to buttress one's own testimony," in the Introduction, George Lamming, *In the Castle of My Skin* (New York: Macmillan Co., Collier Books, 1970), vi.

17. Elizabeth Bowen, "Autobiography as an Art," *The Saturday Review of Literature* (17 March 1951): 9.

18. Edmund A. Steimle, *God the Stranger: Reflections About Resurrection* (Philadelphia: Fortress Press, 1979), 11–16.

19. Martin Luther King, Jr., *Strength to Love* (Philadelphia: Fortress Press, 1981), 106–14.

20. Ibid., 113.

21. Allan Boesak, *Walking on Thorns: The Call to Christian Obedience* (Grand Rapids: Wm. B. Eerdmans, 1984), 42–49.

22. Ibid., 45.

3. ESSENTIAL GUIDELINES
FOR SELF-PORTRAYAL

1. Theodore Ferris, "To Care and Not to Care," in *This Is the Day* (New York: Wilcox & Follett, 1951), 86–87.

2. John Killinger, *Fundamentals of Preaching* (Philadelphia: Fortress Press, 1985), 31.

3. Walter Wangerin, Jr., *Ragman and Other Cries of Faith* (San Francisco: Harper & Row, 1984), 77.

4. Ibid.

5. H. Richard Niebuhr, *The Meaning of Revelation* (New York: Macmillan Co., 1941), 64.

6. Ibid., 65, 60.

7. D. W. Cleverley Ford, *An Expository Preacher's Notebook* (New York: Harper & Brothers, 1960), 20.

8. Leslie D. Weatherhead, *The Significance of Silence and Other Sermons* (Nashville: Abingdon-Cokesbury Press, 1945), 21–29.

9. Fred B. Craddock, *As One Without Authority* (Nashville: Abingdon Press, 1979), 163–68.

10. Ibid., 166.

11. Hans van der Geest, *Presence in the Pulpit: The Impact of Personality in Preaching*, trans. Douglas W. Stott (Atlanta: John Knox Press, 1981), 86.

12. John Navone and Thomas Cooper, *Tellers of the Word* (New York: LeJacq Publishing, 1981), 71–78.

13. Barbara Hardy, "Towards a Poetics of Fiction: (3) An Approach through Narrative," *Novel* 2 (Fall 1968): 9.

14. Tom F. Driver, *Patterns of Grace: Human Experience as Word of God* (San Francisco: Harper & Row, 1977), 133.
15. Michael Goldberg, *Theology and Narrative: A Critical Introduction* (Nashville: Abingdon Press, 1982), 103.
16. Ibid., 106.
17. John Shea, "Theology and Autobiography," *Commonweal* 105 (16 June 1978) 361.
18. Craddock, *As One Without Authority*, 167.
19. Martin Luther King, Jr., *Strength to Love* (Philadelphia: Fortress Press, 1981), 114.
20. Ibid.
21. van der Geest, *Presence in the Pulpit*, 132.
22. Ibid.
23. John R. Claypool, *The Light within You: Looking at Life through New Eyes* (Waco, Tex.: Word, 1983), 133.
24. Ibid.
25. Ibid., 139.
26. Ibid., 140.
27. John R. Fry, *Fire and Blackstone* (Philadelphia: J.B. Lippincott, 1969), 77–84.
28. Ibid., 79.
29. Ibid.
30. Ibid.
31. Ibid., 82.
32. Ibid., 84.

4. SELF-PORTRAYAL AND
THE BIBLICAL TEXT

1. Gustaf Wingren, *The Living Word: A Theological Study of Preaching and the Church*, trans. Victor C. Pogue (Philadelphia: Fortress Press, 1960), 209.
2. Ibid.
3. Ibid., 70–71.
4. Ibid., 68.
5. Ibid., 50.
6. Ibid., 54.
7. Richard Lischer, *A Theology of Preaching: The Dynamics of the Gospel* (Nashville: Abingdon Press, 1981), 19–20, offers helpful suggestions for understanding the preaching task "as broader and more demanding than the serial restatement of a pericope's religious ideas." The last of these suggestions focuses on the text's relation to the "core of the faith."
8. Ibid., 19.
9. Elizabeth Achtemeier, *Preaching as Theology and Art* (Nashville: Abingdon Press, 1984), 15.
10. Helmut Thielicke, *The Waiting Father: Sermons on the Parables of Jesus*,

trans. John W. Doberstein (New York: Harper & Brothers, 1959), 170–81.

11. Ibid., 175.

12. Leslie D. Weatherhead, *The Significance of Silence and Other Sermons* (Nashville: Abingdon-Cokesbury Press, 1945), 21–22.

13. D. W. Cleverley Ford, *An Expository Preacher's Notebook* (New York: Harper & Brothers, 1960), 191–97.

14. John R. Claypool, *Tracks of a Fellow Struggler: How To Handle Grief* (Waco, Tex.: Word, 1978), 41–58.

15. John R. Claypool, *The Light Within You: Looking at Life through New Eyes* (Waco, Tex.: Word, 1983), 131–40.

16. Leslie D. Weatherhead, *When the Lamp Flickers* (Nashville: Abingdon-Cokesbury Press, 1948), 139–50.

17. This sermon appears in Richard L. Thulin, *The Caller and the Called* (Lima, Oh.: CSS of Ohio, 1986), 67–71.

18. Thielicke, *Waiting Father*, 71–82.

19. George W. Stroup, III, "A Bibliographical Critique," *Theology Today* (July 1975): 133.

20. John Shea, "Theology and Autobiography," *Commonweal* 105 (16 June 1978): 362.

21. Elie Wiesel, *Messengers of God: Biblical Portraits and Legends*, trans. Marion Wiesel (New York: Pocket Books, 1977), 12.

22. George W. Stroup, III, *The Promise of Narrative Theology: Recovering the Gospel in the Church* (Atlanta: John Knox Press, 1981), 146. Thomas H. Groome helpfully suggests that there are three sources of teaching and learning in the Christian community as church: "The teaching of the official magisterium, the research of the theologians and scripture scholars, and the discernment of the people (what has been traditionally called the *sensus fidelium*, or the sense of the faithful)," Thomas H. Groome, *Christian Religious Education: Sharing Our Story and Vision* (San Francisco: Harper & Row, 1980), 200.

5. SELF-PORTRAYAL AND THE SERMON

1. I like the claim that the peak moments are given to us so that we may become more capable of hearing the telling of the same story in the "humdrum, the wearisome, and the boring," John Navone and Thomas Cooper, *Tellers of the Word* (New York: LeJacq Publishing, 1981), 62.

2. Frederick Buechner, *The Alphabet of Grace* (New York: Seabury Press, 1981); idem, *The Sacred Journey* (San Francisco: Harper & Row, 1982); and idem, *Now and Then* (San Francisco: Harper & Row, 1983). Madeleine L'Engle, *A Circle of Quiet* (New York: Seabury Press, 1977); idem, *The Summer of the Great-grandmother* (New York: Seabury Press, 1980); and idem, *The Irrational Season* (New York: Seabury Press, 1979). David H. C. Read, *This Grace Given* (Grand Rapids: Wm. B. Eerdmans, 1984).

3. See, e.g., Lois Daniel, *How to Write Your Own Life Story* (Chicago: Chicago Review Press, 1980).

4. See, e.g., Kenneth L. Gibble, *The Preacher as Jacob: A New Paradigm for Preaching* (New York: Seabury Press, 1985), 80–83.

5. See, e.g., William J. Bausch, *Storytelling: Imagination and Faith* (Mystic, Conn.: Twenty-Third Publications, 1984); William R. White, *Speaking in Stories: Resources for Christian Storytellers* (Minneapolis: Augsburg Publishing House, 1982); William R. White, *Stories for Telling: A Treasury for Christian Storytellers* (Minneapolis: Augsburg Publishing House, 1986); and John Gardner, *The Art of Fiction: Notes on Craft for Young Writers* (New York: Vintage Books, 1985).

6. Leslie D. Weatherhead, *When the Lamp Flickers* (Nashville: Abingdon-Cokesbury Press, 1948), 64–72.

7. Ibid., 67.

8. D. W. Cleverley Ford, *An Expository Preacher's Notebook* (New York: Harper & Brothers, 1960), 204–9.

9. Helmut Thielicke, *The Waiting Father: Sermons on the Parables of Jesus*, trans. John W. Doberstein (New York: Harper & Brothers, 1959), 71–82.

10. Ibid., 77.

11. Ibid., 61–70.

12. Theodore Ferris, "To Care and Not to Care," in *This Is the Day* (New York: Wilcox & Follet, 1951), 86–87.

13. In *Preaching Peace*, ed. Ronald J. Sider and Darrel J. Brubaker (Philadelphia: Fortress Press, 1982), 65–69.

14. Ibid., 67.

15. Frank Kermode, "Novel and Narrative," in *The Theory of the Novel: New Essays*, ed. John Halperin (New York: Oxford University Press, 1974), 174.

16. Leslie D. Weatherhead, *That Immortal Sea* (Nashville: Abingdon Press, 1953), 147–57.

17. Edmund A. Steimle, *From Death to Birth* (Philadelphia: Fortress Press, 1973), 3–8.

18. Ibid., 51–56.

6. OCCASIONS FOR SELF-PORTRAYAL

1. Frederick Buechner, *A Room Called Remember* (San Francisco: Harper & Row, 1984), 138.

2. Ibid., 139.

3. Jürgen Moltmann, *The Power of the Powerless: The Word of Liberation for Today*, trans. Margaret Kohl (San Francisco: Harper & Row, 1983), 136.

4. Ibid.

5. Ibid., 136–54.

6. Ibid., 155.

7. P. T. Forsyth, *Positive Preaching and the Modern Mind* (Grand Rapids: Wm. B. Eerdmans, 1966), 192.

8. Ibid., 192–98.

9. Colin Morris, *Mankind My Church* (Nashville: Abingdon Press, 1971), 119.

10. Ibid.

11. D. W. Cleverley Ford, *A Pastoral Preacher's Notebook* (London: Hodder and Stoughton, 1965), 19.

12. Karl Barth, *Deliverance to the Captives*, trans. Marguerite Wieser (New York: Harper & Brothers, 1961), 53.

13. Ibid.

14. Paul Scherer, *The Place Where Thou Standest* (New York: Harper & Brothers, 1942), 83.

15. Buechner, *A Room Called Remember*, 36-45.

16. Ibid., 41.

17. Quoted in John Shea, *Stories of God: An Unauthorized Biography* (Chicago: Thomas More Press, 1978), 57.

18. Moltmann, *The Power of the Powerless*, 142.

19. Ibid.

20. Domenico Grasso, *Proclaiming God's Message: A Study in the Theology of Preaching* (Notre Dame, Ind.: University of Notre Dame Press, 1965), xviii.

21. Robert N. Bellah, Richard Madsen, William M. Sullivan, Ann Swidler, and Steven M. Tipton, *Habits of the Heart: Individualism and Commitment in American Life* (Berkeley and Los Angeles: University of California Press, 1985), 63.

22. Carl E. Braaten, *The Whole Counsel of God* (Philadelphia: Fortress Press, 1974), 73.

23. Helmut Thielicke, *Encounter with Spurgeon*, trans. John W. Doberstein (Greenwood: Attic Press, 1978), 36.

24. Ibid., 38.

25. Since Theilicke has been used as a support, it is only fair to admit that he does not argue for the use of personal story. Quite the contrary, he states that "this coming forward of the witness . . . need not by any means manifest itself in the use of the first person singular or an autobiographical tone of speech," *Encounter with Spurgeon*, 38. And yet he admits that such first-person singular need not be feared (p. 39). He quotes 1 Cor. 3:22, "All things are yours!" And he refers to Augustine's words, "Love, and do what you will!" (p. 40).

26. See the excellent discussion on personal story in "Richard L. Rubenstein, "The Promise and the Pitfalls of Autobiographical Theology," in *Art/Literature/Religion: Life on the Borders*, ed. Robert Detweiler (Chico, Calif.: Scholars Press, 1983), 125–37.

27. *The Human Chain for Divine Grace*, ed. Ronald J. Lavin (Philadelphia: Fortress Press, 1978).

28. Ibid., 43.

29. Ibid., 76.

30. Ibid., 24.

31. Alfred C. Krass, "What the Mainline Denominations Are Doing in Evangelism," *Christian Century* (2 May 1979): 492.

32. Leslie D. Weatherhead, *The Significance of Silence and Other Sermons* (Nashville: Abingdon-Cokesbury Press, 1945), 103.

33. Ibid., 122.

34. Ibid.

35. John R. Claypool, *The Preaching Event* (Waco, Tex.: Word, 1980), 103.

36. Richard A. Jensen, *Telling the Story: Variety and Imagination in Preaching* (Minneapolis: Augsburg Publishing House, 1980), 152.

37. Ronald J. Allen, "Shaping Sermons by the Language of the Text," in *Preaching Biblically: Creating Sermons in the Shape of Scripture*, ed. Don M. Wardlaw (Philadelphia: Westminster Press, 1983), 43.

38. *Preaching in the Witnessing Community*, ed. Herman G. Stuempfle, Jr. (Philadelphia: Fortress Press, 1973), xiv.

39. Ibid., 62–68.

40. Ibid., 67.

DATE DUE			

DEMCO 38-297